# Changing Education to Change the World

## A New Vision of Schooling

# by Claudio Naranjo, M.D.

Consciousness Classics

Gateways Books and Tapes

Nevada City, California

2016

ISBN 978-0-89556-160-2
First Gateways Books edition
Text © 2016 by Claudio Naranjo
Cover Design by Marvette Kort
All Rights Reserved

Published by Gateways Books and Tapes
IDHHB, Inc.
PO Box 370
Nevada City, CA 95959 {USA)
Phone: (800) 869-0658 or (530) 271-2239
E-mail: info@gatewaysbooksandtapes.com
Website: http://www.gatewaysbooksandtapes.com

Library of Congress Cataloging-in-Publication Data

Names: Naranjo, Claudio, 1932- author.
Title: Changing education to change the world : a new approach to schooling /
    by Claudio Naranjo, MD.
Description: Nevada City, California : Gateways Books and Tapes, 2016. |
    Series: Consciousness classics
Identifiers: LCCN 2016042472 | ISBN 9780895561602 (paperback)
Subjects: LCSH: Education--Philosophy. | Transformative learning. |
    Educational change. | BISAC: EDUCATION / Experimental Methods. |
EDUCATION
    / Philosophy & Social Aspects.
Classification: LCC LB14.7 .N35 2016 | DDC 370.1--dc23
LC record available at https://lccn.loc.gov/2016042472

# Table of Contents

## Author's Foreword -- A Note on the English Edition

I am glad that Gateways is publishing this English translation of the first part of a book of mine that was published nine years ago in Spain and has also appeared in Italian, Russian and Portuguese.

At first it was received as the work of a newcomer to the field of education, but in time it has inspired two universities to grant me an honorary doctorate in education and probably contributed to my nomination for a Nobel Peace Prize as well as the invitation to join the Advisory Board of the Global Education Futures Forum. More than that, it has paved the way for my becoming an influential voice among the teachers of a number of countries, who have come to share in my conviction that only by changing consciousness may we expect social evolution, and only by making education relevant to psycho-spiritual development could we expect a massive change in consciousness.

I have suggested to Iven Lourie, Editor at Gateways, the addition of some more recent essays on an education geared to the healing of the Patriarchal mind, which I take to be the unacknowledged root of our individual pathologies and also of our ever-worsening social problems; but he tells me that it is too late for that, and it will be more appropriate to include such a supplement in an e-book. I look forward, then, to that additional publication, and take this opportunity to let my readers know about it.

May this little book contribute to our time of deep social transformation, as the dying patriarchal system that we created some thousands of years ago gives way to the emergence of a healthy society—where children's pleasure drive is no longer criminalized and women's empathic spirit no longer eclipsed by the hegemonic and predatory spirit of an excessively individualistic and competitive masculine world.

Claudio Naranjo
July, 2016

## 1. For a Salvific Education

### The Promise of a Dying Civilization

Patriarchy is a historic creation made by men and women and formed over some 2500 years. In its earliest form it appeared as the archaic state. The basic unit of organization was the patriarchal family, which expressed and generated, step by step, its own rules and values.

Gerda Lerner, *The Creation of the Patriarchy*

Seen from close up, the conquering of the world is not a pretty thing.

Joseph Conrad

The more man has been subject to collective norms, the more individually immoral he has become.

Carl Jung

**M**uch has been said about "our historical moment" at this end of millennium, be it with a catastrophic attitude or with the enthusiasm appropriate to the change of millennium, and it is difficult to ignore the relevance of the apocalyptic vision of our times, and there is no doubt that we are attending a cultural crisis that seems headed toward collapse, and yet it is also healthy to entertain a certain optimism, born of hope and faith in human destiny.

Marx had already written about how internal contradictions of capitalism would cause a crisis in an intrinsically exploitive social system. But it has only been recently that we have realized that our society is effectively in a crisis, and not so much because of economic or financial failure, for now, but as a result of the exploitation of nature.

The report entitled "Limits to Growth," conducted for the Club of Rome by the Stanford Research Institute, first showed that we are in danger of extinction in the same manner that the dinosaurs millions of years ago became extinct, because of our inflexibility; and even though there are academics that argue that those predictions have not come to pass, that is not completely true, and we recognize in the Club of Rome the clearest vision of what we could call our objective problem. I use the term "objective problem" to distinguish it from the underlying psycho-spiritual problem, which I see and which will be my topic, and in using the term "problem" I do so (as does the Club of Rome) in reference to a set of problems that are in such a way interrelated that the isolated solution, which has gotten away from specialists, demands a systemic approach—since what is good for solving one problem sometimes ends up making the solution to another more difficult.

The Encyclopedia of Problems and Human Resources, published years ago by Humanité 2001 in Belgium, lists more than 8000 problems, but it is clear that many of them are old. Among the new problems, three stand out, starting with overpopulation. We could say that overpopulation makes old problems not only more current but also more severe: there are so many people in the world that we can no longer continue to live in the same way. We have many bad habits that at one time didn't matter. For example, there was a time when we could throw the garbage "a little farther away," but we can't do that anymore because there is no "little farther away." Sending radioactive waste into space is being considered, since here on Earth our neighbors are closer every day. There used to always be a new place to conquer, and that allowed mankind to manifest the hunger for conquest that is so characteristic of our civilization—which Toynbee called Faust-like in an implicit allusion to the last scene of Goethe's Faust. In this work Faust feels that he is a benefactor of humanity when, with the help of Mephistopheles, he insists on building dikes that allow him to take land from the sea.

A second new situation (also brought to mind by the cited scene from Faust) is technological progress which, like overpopulation, amplifies and causes many characteristic attitudes which have been expressed in the way we live collectively since the very beginning of civilization. It's not only that we're using up non-renewable natural resources or about the danger of self-destructing in war: we're interfering with the balance of nature in such a way that we participate in the disappearing of forests and in the poisoning of marine plankton on which depends the renewal of the oxygen we breathe, and we are threatened by the gradual heating of the atmosphere because of the accumulation of carbon anhydride. This, in turn, could be followed by the melting of polar caps and the flooding of large sections of the inhabited world—beginning with the ports.

To this we must add the progressive destruction of the ozone layer which protects us from the ultra-violet radiation of the sun, not only contributing to warming, but also giving way to lethal levels of said radiation. If we also consider the animal species that disappear each day, we can't help but to feel anxious as a result of constant human interference in the complex diversity which is life, especially when we take into account that the phenomenons that seem to have caused the massive extinction of certain species in other geological eras were similar in nature.

A third eminently modern problematic factor is the effect transnational companies and large accumulations of money are having on government and nongovernmental organizations—with their respective initiatives. We live in a world that is largely ruled by purely economic criteria, while in ancient times politics at least aspired to serve other values. It is true that much blood has been shed because of diverse nationalistic causes and the thought of overcoming a world divided by sovereign states could inspire optimism, but it is not only the sovereign states that see their free determination threatened: the entire world seems to have become a simple market for jobs and products in which human needs and cultural values that have been considered universal have been smothered bit by bit. I would like to include some eloquent lines from the report about poverty in the world that a few years ago appeared in *Practical Guides* from Aguilar editorial:

New forms of economical control and ways to dominate people are developed worldwide, planned by large multinational corporations, the most powerful nations of the world, and certain international organisms. The distance between North and South grows greater every day. Scientific knowledge is controlled by a few. Economic, financial, commercial, technological, political and military power is concentrated and centralized in the hands of a few people.

Faced with these changes, a huge number of the men and women who populate the Earth look at their present and look to their near future with little hope. Poverty and hunger in the world has increased. The majority of the population is ever more excluded from decision-making in their own lives and their own future. Access to basic needs is more and more limited: property, land, the use of goods, technological advance, health, and education.

Models of political, economic and socio-cultural organization have been forced on society, destined to break down culture belonging to communities, and create absolute dependency on and servitude to the strongest, expecting who knows what kind of future. The United Nations report, *"Human Development 1994,"* confirms that while the difference between the 20% of the richest people in the world and the poorest people in the world was 30 to 1 in 1960, by 1994 this proportion had reached 60 to 1.

But, as I've said, we have spoken so much about our historical moment during the last decades and my topic for these pages is our psycho-historical moment. As a person whose specific experience is in the areas of spirituality and therapy—in other words the material that has to do with human development—I will not talk about our objective problem so much as of the configuration of that problem's interior aspects; in other words, not so much about the technocratic-commercial system that defines us as the "Great Beast" of the prophecy, but about our heart—meaning the psychological and spiritual aspects of our collective illness.

When speaking of a psycho-historical approach, I am not only referring to the fact that I will discuss the internal aspect of our problems, but also of an attempt to understand what is happening in the world today from the perspective of cultural evolution. And since the word "culture" is generally understood as a relatively external factor—making allusion to ideas, painting, musical works, customs, institutions, and so on—it is necessary to state that my interest lies in the history of the "human spirit." I am interested then in the consideration of our time and our history with a focus on the psychological or mental aspects, and I will invite my readers to observe the parallelism between our historical development and the development of the individual conscience.

Personally I feel a certain fascination for the idea that in different sectors of reality we can see similar processes, laws or structures although science has not shown us what the causal relationships among these cases of "isomorphism" is exactly. A very well known example is how the evolution of the species repeats itself—evolution that has taken place throughout successive geological ages—in the life of an individual. Each of us began our life as a unicellular organism and went through the embryonic stage that is reminiscent of the life of invertebrates. Later, as vertebrates, we were a little like fish. Then there was a moment in the development of the embryo in which we were a lot like mice, since our evolutionary lineage went through a rodent stage before going through the stage of insect eaters, all this before monkeys when the cerebral cortex began to develop in its relation to the eye and the hand. In summary our individual development is an echo of the evolution of our species.

But even more mysterious is the echo between different levels of reality. For example: Is it a coincidence that in the world of sound the duplication of a frequency of sound defines the musical octave—in which notes are repeated eight by eight in such a way that the progressive ascent becomes a spiral—when in the visual world the colors in the visible spectrum also make up an octave? And according to the periodic table of Mendeleyeff the chemical elements also form octaves? Our intuition tells us that there is a universal structure and this, without a doubt, has made some feel as if the Creator had put his fingerprint on certain parts of creation. It also seems to us that music is a sonorous mirror of universal law, and it has been said that it brings to existence a "music of the spheres." When we listen to the music of Beethoven, for example, we strongly feel that it reflects living processes: the spiral structure of its temporal configuration reminds us of a familiar development from our affective experience. It seems as though after the Baroque period, when music was linear, the human experience of development was fused into it, and in this way the musical expression of the laws of life itself was found.

We can, in a very abstract way, speak of these morphological echoes in terms of a fractal structure in the universe. For those who are new to this recent mathematical term, an image can provide us with a simple explanation: the image of a man looking at a bottle on which there is a man looking at a bottle on which there is...etc. Or we could take the image of mirrors that reflect each other infinitely. In both cases, a part reflects the whole, and this situation, far from being exclusive to human invention, can be something that appears generally in the organization of the natural world. So, for example, in trees arborization is seen in the structure of the trunk from which the main branches sprout. The same is seen in each branch and lastly in the nerve structure of each leaf. Even in each branch of each nerve the entire form of the tree is repeated.

Personally, as I have said before, I am very interested in the idea of a fractal structure or holographic structure of the world and what I propose to do here is to explore a particular case of isomorphism, the idea of society as an organism: the idea that states that our collective organism has an evolution and that that evolution can, perhaps, have characteristics that are similar to those we recognize in isolated individual development.

The idea was proposed by Spencer, a sociologist who worked in Darwin's shadow. And perhaps because what he proposed was "social Darwinism," in which was suggested the desire to justify incipient capitalistic industrialism through the idea of survival of the fittest in natural order, that the idea he also proposed of a social organism with its own laws did not become very popular in his time. More recently the idea of a potentially organismic society seems to be appearing in our culture—as the holistic paradigm becomes prominent and system sciences like ecology with its concept of Gaya (the Earth as a living organism) come to the forefront. Modern science is no longer in a hurry to eradicate the assumed superstition in the hermetic saying: "as it is above it is below." The same idea that states that between the atomic level and the planetary level of the inorganic world there is a certain analogy seems to support the idea that in the social level of human life certain characteristics can be observed that are similar to those of the individual.

I believe that great promise presented by the idea of isomorphism between the evolution of individual consciousness and the evolution of culture throughout history is that we know more about individual evolution than we do about social evolution, since through the years there have always been individuals that have "crossed the river," individuals that have reached what we can only call the promise of human potential.

The Greeks recognized a divine potential in human beings, a potential which is celebrated by the myth and culture of Dionysius, divine son of God who became mortal and survived his own death. In a more ample sense, this superhuman man who became divine and transcended death was called a hero, and the cult to the heroes in Greece was more solemn than the cult to the gods—since it involved mourning their tragic deaths and the expectation of blessings that emanated from those same deaths.

Heroes have shared their lives with us through generations, no matter what we call them, and it's difficult not to see that throughout history there have been beings such as the creators of religions and other religious geniuses, saints or teachers that had something to tell us about the process through which they reached wisdom and kindness. The luminaries of human consciousness throughout all civilizations have transmitted highly sophisticated ideas about what the road is like and psychology now has begun to feed on these ancient sources.

Transpersonal psychology has shown an interest in integrating the information that scientific observation gives us about the first phases of development with the information that the ancient ones had always known about the more advanced phases of "the journey of transformation." And one thing is clear: the process of evolution of individual consciousness is a type of psycho-spiritual metamorphosis that involves a process of death and rebirth. We go through many small psychological deaths through which we leave behind certain motivations and we begin to let go of aspects of our personality forged during childhood, from falseness, which is a part of the social pathology that surrounds us and that we've internalized, or the ideas we've adopted as a method of defense, and as we let go and free ourselves from that which is obsolete and limiting, our internal potential emerges, the higher consciousness that we call our spirit and which is like a flower that blossoms on the tree of our lives. Using the language of transpersonal psychology, we leave behind our ego and begin to free our essential selves from the prison of our "neurotic" conditioned compulsiveness.

All of this happens in phases. It starts in puberty which is the moment in which we reach a small liberation, when it seems that something new is born into human life. Naturally our development has gone through many stages before that, from the phase called separation/ individuation in which we start depending less on contact with our mother and exploring the surroundings more autonomously, to the important stage at 6 to 7 years old during which our intellect acquires greater capacity for abstraction and which is the stage in which, for many, the part of childhood that they remember begins. But during these early transitions in infancy what happens is a combination of maturing, socializing and perturbing of our original health: as our faculties mature we progressively enter the world and fall progressively from paradise. Then in puberty "the road home" begins, the beginning of the transformation—even though for many, perhaps for most, this process becomes detained. Many people feel as if they had been born during adolescence, or had finished being born— although in the perspective of life lived it may be more exact to say that it is the first in a series of births that will take place during the process of progressive individualization that coincides with the progressive deepening of relationships. It seems as if it is only then that a truly personal "I" begins to exist—an independent third person—in the world of the internalizations of father and mother.

And the beginning of adolescence holds a crisis: a difficult period of transition. It is the first in a series of difficult transitions that will come about during the life of the person—one of many qualitative jumps in our process of development that come together with delicate passages.

At the entrance to adult life, meaning the time in which we are said to have entered "the age of majority," many people recognize another critical moment. Certainly this transition, like puberty, includes biological maturing. It is now (at about 24 or 25 years old) that skeletal ossification is finished, and the fact that it is just before this that we are given freedoms and responsibilities of adulthood implies the recognition of psychological maturity as well. For many this is a time in which the young adult leaves the family of origin and, for those who had the opportunity to study a career, it is the time of transition from preparatory learning to service and work. Leaving things behind is like dying a little bit, just as when the individual begins to live a more creative and individual life it is like being born. Again the individual changes worlds, and upon distancing himself from the original influences there may be a loss of interest in contact with previous friends. The person feels that life will now truly begin and that before this he really didn't understand anything. He may feel that there has been much advance and growth in his life, even to the point that college friends may now be despised.

Later on in life there is a third critical period around 36 or 37 years of age: the stage is frequently referred to as a middle aged crisis. Perhaps it was Jung who first realized that around the middle of life many people feel that what they have been doing is no longer satisfactory for them, and it seems that the same success that they have had in reaching their adolescent expectations will take them to discover the limitations of those satisfactions and purposes. More decisively, disappointment in old dreams and ideals opens them up to an inner search that, independently from religious influence, could be called a conversion, through which the person distances himself from the mundane to take the first steps on a deliberate path to evolution.

There seems to be a 12-year cycle throughout our development, in such a way that the transition at puberty (at 12) and adulthood (at 24) continues with the transition at midlife (at 36). It's interesting to note that approximately at this age some enter a path, others (like Buddha or Whitman) have reached spiritual maturity or found (thinking of Mozart, Byron, Schubert, Keats and others), after blossoming early, death.

Just as critical as the transition from infancy to adolescence that is often accompanied by suffering and problems, and as the era of transition into adult life which is also a moment in which psychological problems can reach the severity of psychosis, the transition that follows can coincide with the height of individual problems. I would say that this is the time of life in which individual neurosis, which evolves in people whose mind and body have been brought up to sustain a parasitic existence, reaches maximum development and a point at which it can no longer be ignored. It is the time of life, for example, in which an obsessive personality reaches such a level of obsessiveness that there is nothing left to do but understand the illness or vehemently propose a change of course. It's also the time at which an alcoholic succumbs to his addiction to the extreme in which family life and survival in itself become threatened. But it is precisely this deepening of emotional and personality problems that drives the person into an effective therapeutic process or to the beginning of true spiritual work.

Although the idea that there are biological cycles of approximately 12 years in our development is confirmed by the fact that at approximately 48 menopause begins and at 60 old age begins, these are not the most significant stages from the point of view of the development of consciousness, for whoever has lived this change of direction "at the middle of life's road" sooner or later will gather up the first fruits of the search. Particularly when a person feels sufficiently motivated to seek help from a psychotherapist or any of the traditional spiritual schools, the stage of being a candidate (of the *vía purgativa* in Christian mysticism) will give way to the enlightened path—a time of harvesting and abundance that constitutes once more—and more than ever—a birth: a birth of the spirit or a birth unto the spirit.

But not even this phase of expanded consciousness constitutes the end to internal development, since the illuminative phase sooner or later leads to the contraction of consciousness that in the Christian world is known as "the dark night of the soul"—the *nigredo* or blackness of the alchemists—which is at the same time a period of incubation and internal death: that which St. Paul alluded to when speaking of the death of "the old man" which comes before the birth of the new man. Few get to know this "dark night" that makes up the next and deepest crisis in human development, but I think that what we know about it (through the experience of those few who, like Jonah, were swallowed and vomited up) is of interest not only (like always) to pilgrims who are on an inner journey, but to all—because of its relevance to our collective situation. Since, as I would like to share throughout the next pages, I think that that which in the development of individual consciousness is the dark time that comes before the definitive stage of the maturing of the spirit, known in mystical theology as the "via unitiva," is where we find the most adequate paradigm for the stage of collective evolution which we are going through today.

But what I would like to propose presupposes the consideration of history in its totality and its stages. Is it true that we can discern leaps or critical analogous transitions which can be observed in individual development? And do the notions of death and birth clarify the historical process?

In the psycho-spiritual evolution of an individual the idea of transitions that include characteristics of birth and death is important because, in spite of the connotation of the word "individual," our mind is dual: far from being unified beings, we have inside us, along with our essential being, a kind of parasitic sub-personality that we can call our neurosis. (I'm very sorry to see the word "neurosis" disappearing from modern psychiatric language, since we need some term to refer to the fact that the majority of syndromes known by psychopathology are alternate manifestations of a similar illness, and not a true multiplicity.) We could say that we have two "I's" in each of us - one healthy and the other (an echo of collective illness) sick. Based on that, our early development becomes the maturing of our essential being and the growth of our parasitic being—in other words, a complication and strengthening of our psychopathology. Later, when in the best of cases we begin recovering our health, we can say that the sick part of ourselves begins to die and that our healthy part, free from interference, peeks out or is born.

Applied to our collective condition this idea could solve the paradox and the undeniable observation that our history holds both progress and decadence: we progress in knowledge and dominion over the world, but collective evil also evolves—from which we are barely now freeing ourselves—like when faced with a partially annihilated enemy that calls for backup and that we've not yet finished defeating.

It seems clear that at the beginning of our history, like at the beginning of our individual lives, we developed in a traumatic atmosphere. The trauma which each child faced upon leaving the mother's womb was invisible to us until recently, just as water is invisible to the fish that moves in it. The universality and the antiquity of our condition had accustomed us and in a certain way had silenced our soul. In our time of elevated ecological consciousness, nevertheless, it has become evident for many that what Reich called "the emotional plague" is transmitted through generations as the original sin. At least people who go through a therapeutic process come to see the wounds of infancy and the origin of these wounds in the characterological aberrations of their parents—and understanding this has been enough to provoke the understanding that the defects of the parents, in turn, have been echoes of the limitations of the loving capabilities of their respective parents as well—and so on. In the same way that an individual suffers and becomes ill (knowingly or not) because of anguish, frustration and insecurity caused by the encounter with the aberrant emotional condition found in his surroundings, it is difficult to doubt that the first humans suffered the trauma of severe threats to survival: the history of our species began during the last glacier era, when the threat of cold joined the threat of hunger, and the need to survive in such precarious conditions surely brought on the need to kill—perhaps even other humans.

And this is very paradoxical. History can be read simultaneously in two ways. As a continual progression, like Darwinians want to read it, which through to the 50s—not long ago—was the predominant view, or according to another point of view which coincides with the ancient reading of spiritual traditions. According to this we've fallen from an archaic paradise-like condition, and we are not finished falling: we are falling through the ages, and our scientific progress is inserted in an increasingly dehumanized context.

Spengler showed how all great civilizations were born in glory and after a seminal golden age reached their splendorous summer when all their potentialities flourished, after which a long period of decadence began until their winter arrived when they went through atrophy and fossilization. Later Toynbee wrote his extensive *Study of History* which was highly acclaimed in his time, although now it is not so popular because historians consider it commonplace that, as he so clearly showed, civilizations are born in answer to challenges and with time die. At times there are matches, as in our civilization, which is a hybrid of double origin: our civilization is the prolongation of the Greco-Roman world, and we could say that this world mothered us, but the Greco-Roman world was fertilized by the Judeo-Christian world, and although our genes have come to us mainly from Indo-Europeans, our spirit (in spite of the characteristic anti-Semitism of the European Society) has come to us mainly from Abraham.

But coming back to the considerations of the dawn of history: I was saying that just as happens in individual life, our earliest evolution coincided with the maturing of our faculties in highly traumatic circumstances. So in the same way that we individually fell from paradise into a womb and then into this world headfirst, having a bad time of it straight out in the delivery room of some hospital (where we were slapped on the back with the lack of sensitivity characteristic of our culture in order to confirm by our screams that we were alive), in our collective lives we have also fallen "headfirst." Even though the challenge of this fall from abundance and tropical jungle life into precariousness has been a stimulus for astuteness and the practical intelligence that we now see bearing fruit in the form of the development of technology, we've also lost something in that necessary hardening. I think it's convenient to understand the development of history as a plant that has been contaminated by a parasite: as it grows, the parasite that feeds on it also grows. So as our being evolves through history, our sickness also evolves, like cancer does today.

In individual life, in order to overcome dysfunctional programming that our symptoms and difficulties in relationships depend on, we have to go back to the original trauma—that is not always a precise incident, but it is often a permanent situation from which we had to learn to defend ourselves by adopting a false identity and betraying our true selves. It is said that history helps us to understand the present, and I think that it is also possible to cure our collective alienation through understanding and reconsidering our original historical trauma, which was no other than that first threat of hunger and cold that taught us to kill our own kind to survive. The scarce remains from the dawn of our history as Homo sapiens suggest that our ancestors, the Cro-Magnon, must have learned to eat not only large animals like polar bears, but also their own cousins, the Neanderthal. The extinction of the Neanderthal man at that time and the notable proportion of perforated craniums among the remains suggest that we had to become cannibals—and that helps us to understand the cannibalistic phenomenon in recent times as a remainder of necessary and sanctified cannibalism in ancient times.

Is very interesting to consider how religion in its origins was intimately tied to sacrifice, first human sacrifice and later animal sacrifice, which later gave way to symbolic sacrifice and the psychological concept of the sacrifice of one's self. Recently much attention has been paid by anthropologists and historians to the book by René Girard titled *The Violent and the Sacred* which was written with the objective of understanding the relationship between violence and religion as a result of the sanctification of an original or archaic crime. I don't share the interpretations of Gerard. I think that we must have had to break our original link with those like us and betray and impoverish our original loving potential in the dawn of our history. And I think that it helps us to understand both the original trauma of our species and the origin of rites of sacrifice, a custom observed not so long ago by the Eskimos who, after breeding a polar bear as a domestic loved animal, prepared for its happy transition toward a better life before sacrificing it and eating it. It's not difficult to empathetically understand the psychological situation of having to reconcile love with the need to kill to survive. The sacrificial rite, we could say, is a way to decriminalize unavoidable violence through compensation that is both sanctifying and expiatory. As time passes, nevertheless, we have become accustomed to considering ourselves the owners of creation and to trivializing death, not only of animals, but—particularly during the era of television —of humans. All of this favors the persistence of the crypto-cannibalistic attitude that has been characteristic of our history of violent exploitation and has been felt so dramatically in the current exterminating greed of global capitalistic imperialism, which is destroying nature, the dispossessed, and human values. The voraciousness of ancient times and human insensitivity make it easy to understand why throughout history there have been few thinkers who have considered humankind to be intrinsically loving. Surely we have not behaved as kind beings throughout our collective history, and realists have not been able to ignore this fact. But I think that the faith that Rousseau had in our intrinsic kindness anticipated the general vision of modern psychology and reflected a more acute psychological understanding than the cynicism of Machiavelli: today we can see how prophetic his idea was when he said that we are prisoners of civilization and must return in some way to an archaic condition. Salvador Paniker was right then in proposing a retro-progressive evolution in which advancing implies recovering something primitive that we've lost.

The next step—or chapter—in our history was the step that took us into competitive anarchy (as Darwin had imagined as a result of natural selection of the species) or what has been called the Neolithic era in reference to the archaeological finds of tools and weapons made out of polished stone. But more important even than technical progress in stone working was the transition from a nomadic lifestyle to a sedentary lifestyle, which was made possible when man began to cultivate vegetables. This transition is often called "the agricultural revolution," but this expression falls short in the understanding of a much deeper change, since not only was agriculture born at that time but, culture itself: the first tombs not only indicate a consciousness of death, but also the veneration of the dead in which can be appreciated the concept of a beyond. Other signs tell us that during this time—between 30 and 10 thousand years ago—the religious spirit was born. And art was born—

as seen today in the magnificent cave paintings found in Lascaux and other caves, as well as objects carved in stone and ivory. Pottery working began and the first textiles came about. Above and beyond all such specific inventions (which include agriculture, houses, clothes, pottery, and basket weaving) there is also an obvious common spirit in cultivating and caretaking, as if cultivating the land was nothing more than the extension of human cultivation and caretaking and as if homes and clothing, like the caves themselves, were simple projections of the mother's womb in the external world. Although those who study the subject have not come to a totally unanimous agreement, it seems that a sedentary lifestyle and the agricultural revolution were feminine initiatives, and the finding of many feminine figures among the archaeological remains is coherent with this idea—figures with prominent bellies and breasts that suggest homage paid to procreation and maternity. This began the Neolithic era—at least in the basin of the Mediterranean Sea and in the Middle East—today some call it the matristic era.

It was Bachofen, notable contemporary historian and colleague of Nietzsche in the Basilea University, who, toward the end of the 19th century, for the first time came up with the idea that some institutions and uses considered to be a simple expression of human nature should really be considered part of a relatively recent patriarchal culture, before which would have existed a matriarchal culture. By analyzing texts (like those of Herodotus) and artifacts, he observed that there was a time when culture was centered on the figure of women and that masculine values (warrior heroism) depended on feminine values (cultivating and affirming life). So in Greece, for example, before the time of the Olympic gods, religious life was dominated by the figure of the great mother goddess, and this different religion was associated to other priorities in the area of law and a different property regime—in which said property, like names, were handed down through the mother's lineage. Bachofen's idea became an enormous stimulus for the development of anthropology, which at first was greatly interested in investigating contemporary matriarchal cultures.

The results of this research was carefully analyzed in an ample work written by Robert Briffault, although we can say that, according to some, the information collected was not sufficient to validate the idea of a matriarchal culture; but although the domination of women or the feminine should not be taken as analog to masculine domination—since domination through force is something that only came about with the supremacy of man, and even though it is true that there have been no important examples of matriarchal cultures found, etymologically speaking, of a "feminine" government, there are many matristic cultures in which the power of the feminine is expressed through the dignity and influence of women and the prominence of feminine values. Among these, the most characteristic, together with the reverence for life and the sacredness of procreation, to me seems to be tribal solidarity.

Although, according to the agreement among historians, the agricultural revolution of the Neolithic era precedes by thousands of years the birth of the first civilizations, it was at this time, during which the presence of women seemed to soften and add emotional depth to the lives of the first nomadic hunters, when the movement toward civilization became present and blossomed with the advent of the first large cities.

We could well say that not only was culture itself born during the matristic era, but man himself was born then. It is then when the human animal effectively became a cultural animal. In the language of *Genesis* we could say that this is the time of Adam in history, the time when the spirit was breathed into mankind. And if we look for an analogy for this phase of maturity, which at the same time was a time of socialization and culturalization for our species, we find in this transition the greater maturity and socialization that takes place during the second childhood.

In this case we can also see a certain softening of instinctive reactions barely inhibited in the first infancy—the characteristic inhibition that Freud called "period of latency"—and for most people the life lived previously, as if it were a personal prehistorical time, becomes forgotten.

But after Adam came Cain and, according to the brief words from the Bible story of Cain and Abel, that era was not only the time during which, having been expelled from Paradise, we were initiated into criminal activity, but also into the metal age.

It is this new transition in the history of our culture that ends prehistorical times and begins history as we know it today—this is the time of the so-called "urban revolution" and also the time in which we invented the alphabet, and with the alphabet we began to explicitly record our acts and thoughts.

The Ice Age was apparently followed by an age during which melting ice caused floods and rains—the "flood" of so many ancient legends. But then it began to dry and peoples grouped together near large rivers: the rivers of Mesopotamia; the Nile, the Yangtze, the Ganges. On the edges of these rivers large groups of humans had to cultivate the land, and to coordinate their efforts they instituted a system of hierarchical authority on a large scale. The fact that it was a benign authority is suggested by the fact and the reasoning that the first governors were priest-kings who did not own land: we know that among the Sumerians the owners of the land were the gods while the priest-kings were only their intermediaries and servants. But we also know that authority is a very delicate thing and, as has been repeated since Lord Acton observed it, "authority corrupts and absolute authority leads to total corruption." In other words: where there is greater authority there is greater danger that the authority come to serve personal interests that are in conflict with the common good. There's really no need to point out how, in the course of history, this has been shown time and again, that benign authority becomes authoritarianism, that under an authoritative regime those who have the passion to give orders do so, and the interests created feed the thirst for power.

The era that follows the matristic age has been characterized by Ken Wilber as a solar age and the historical development of consciousness. This is justified not only by the noteworthy cultural advance that brought about important inventions like writing and the calendar, but also the fact that great temples suggest spiritual advance: to the ancient religion of the Earth is added now the religion of the heavens—in other words: the institution of transcendental sacredness.

But we cannot ignore the problematic part of the birth of patriarchal society: only then do wars start and with this new regime slavery also begins.

It is probable that slavery began with the kidnapping of women. Just as Hollywood movies show us the story of the Huns and other primitive Aryans, hordes of warriors would fall upon sedentary populations and take the women for reproduction and domestic servants. Later, the powerful victors seemed to have realized that more generalized slavery could be possible and convenient: not only could women be captured and sold but men could be as well.

Since from slavery to the establishment of social classes there's only a small step, we can understand original violence toward women as the origin of the permanent establishment of an oppressed class - and also of an oppressing class which gives itself the right to govern over the other "for its own good."

There are indications that the establishment of a patriarchal regime brought about violent revolutions, as is suggested in different myths, like the one that tells how Apollo, after having defeated the serpent Python, replaces her with the Oracle of Delphi, or the myth of Perseus, Greek hero, which tells the story of how, with the help of Hermes and Pallas Athena, he beheads the terrible Gorgon. The Gorgon—like Python, a personification of the great mother Goddess—had hair in the form of serpents, which suggests her relationship with the archaic world of instinct. (The association of the archaic goddess with the serpent is universal, as well as the fact that the patriarchal world becomes an enemy of the serpent, which reflects the replacement of a religion based on Earth and life by a religion based on heaven and transcendence.)

It is understandable that feminism today has a tendency to identify the matristic era with the legendary lost paradise; however, I'm inclined to think that the vision of the ancient ones who conceived this time—the mythical silver age —as the first phase deterioration from the previous condition of original harmony alluded to as a golden era is more exact. This is suggested by the association of matristic cultures with human sacrifice and also the regime of group tyranny. Erich Fromm has interpreted this phase and collective development of our consciousness as a time in which we were stuck in incestuous union with Earth, and I suspect that the revolution through which the masculine and the hunters took over power was felt as a liberating gesture in favor of the evolution of human potential and against the limitations of the status quo.

It is more than possible then that the patriarchal revolution, in spite of the criminal violence that it injected our culture with, did respond to a need—constituting, as did our original anthropophagy, a sacred crime. The fact that it could have been that way, nevertheless, does not mean that the patriarchal regime is still necessary; today it is necessary that we completely understand the destructive obsolescence of the patriarchal civilization, and while it is true that the structure of the process of individual transformation can be applied to the collective consciousness—a process that requires comprehension and reconsideration of past wounds and the corresponding forms of early reactivity in our attitude toward the world, which have become automatic and unconscious—it is indispensable that we understand that since remote times the way of living that we've considered correct has not been functional or loving. What's more: they should be revised and we should open ourselves to the possibility that we have been wrong. Just like nothing helps an individual more than understanding what happened at the beginning of his or her own life in order to take steps toward liberation, I now think that we need to consider that our common problems today are nothing more than the natural development of what's been happening through millennia.

And it isn't simply about capitalism or the mentality that came about with the industrial age, nor is it simply something that complicated our lives during the last centuries: it's about something as ancient as our civilization itself, and we can call it "the deep structure" of that which began 4 to 5 millennia ago during what was called "the Bronze Age." Such is the nature of our "crisis," a term which, as indicated by the often mentioned hexagram from the *I Ching*, holds both danger and opportunity. And discovering that—beyond authoritarianism, violence, nationalism, mercantilism and other evils that are just as undeniable as well known—the fundamental evil that affects us is found in the patriarchal structure of our minds and our relationships, which invites us to think that we have become fixated in an adolescent stage of collective consciousness even though today such immaturity is becoming unsustainable.

But let's continue with the consideration of the analogies between the evolution of an individual and stages in history. If puberty or the first adolescence of our species was the heroic "Bronze Age" in which masculine domination was instituted through violence and astuteness, we can say that we collectively reached the age of majority with the later development of the patriarchal society that was characterized by the first empires: an age that in mythology and archaeology is designated as "the Iron Age." And if in the matristic "Silver Age" during which we became sedentary farmers corresponds to the "Edenistic" period of our biblical myth, and the transition to the Bronze Age is signaled in the same myth by Cain—the first metallurgist—the Iron Age is the age of Nimrod, which continues into the age of giants and of the growing perversion which characterizes the times between Babel and the flood.

But the biblical story is a mosaic in which various previous stories are integrated and historians tell us that, allegories aside, it is the conquest of Canaan that corresponds to the Bronze Age, and that the Iron Age in the history of Israel corresponds to the times of King David and Solomon—

during the time that the so-called *"books of Moses"* were written.

In Greece, the Iron Age begins with the war of Troy, and in India with the war between Pandavas and Kauravas which is the topic of the Mahabharata. The Iron Age is also the time of the first Mesopotamian empires—the time of the legendary Gilgamesh and his excesses. The Greeks of the time of Homer exalted Achilles and Ulysses but also conceived their time as less clear than the time when the greater number of semi-God heroes had lived. In these cases and in the case of the Babylonians and Egyptians it could be said the greatness of the heroic Bronze Age was complicated by a larger grandiosity. Joseph Campbell invented the expression "mystic inflation" in reference to the attitude that caused Egyptians to bury their pharaohs along with their families and servants—suffocated in their graves, in an act of total devotion. This practice shows more than just a simple hierarchy of spiritual power, a type of drunkenness in power that has turned unnecessarily against life. We could say that, just like in individual psychology, grandiosity hid insecurity and the need to reestablish power that is threatened or whose legitimacy is in doubt.

If the Bronze Age with its patriarchal revolution constituted puberty for our species, we could say that the Iron Age—with its destructive surge of violent power—corresponded to this second adolescence that we call "the age of majority."

But I had said that in our individual development adulthood can be followed (in the best of cases) by another critical transition that is associated to the de-idealization of our adolescent dreams upon starting in a new direction. This is what has been called "midlife crisis," made up by "the entrance crisis" to the path itself: initiation, conversion or metanoia.

When this crisis appears, we pass the threshold that leads to a process of self-knowledge and self-realization in which all the values of the adult world seem to become obsolete, and from the will to leave behind what is known

comes a flight: a first approximation to the spiritual experience
or contemplative experience itself. The conscience of the
seeker is born and the internal journey is begun, going higher
and deeper each time.

We can find something like this also in the process of
social evolution. After the age of our bloody adulthood,
during the degenerate patriarchy, comes a time in history that
Jaspers has called "the axial period" because it appears to be
collective metanoia.

So just as in the beginning when civilizations came
about in a synchrony that makes us consider the unique
network of consciousness (whether in this world or through
their participation with the invisible), the synchrony of
cultures in the time of Zoroaster, the Upanishads, Buddha,
Confucius, Lao Tse or Socrates also draws our attention.
Although, in his push to find an analogy in the history of the
Jewish people some 500 years before Christ, Jaspers points to
Isaiah, it seems more reasonable to find the true parallel in
Jesus Christ, in spite of the time difference—understandable in
a culture that persisted for such a long time in the pastoral way
of life. In the legend of the Jewish people, nevertheless, the
blossoming of knowledge that comes after the Iron Age is
symbolized by Noah, and the same transition is echoed in the
story of the migration of Abraham of Chaldea, which
continues with the description of the development of the
prophetic mind throughout the history of Abraham and the
other patriarchs.

It would seem that the axial period constitutes the
equivalent of the illuminative phase of our collective
evolution, but it is much more exact to compare it to the
epiphany that comes before the path—like the star that shows
the way to the manger or the burning bush on Sinai. It is the
illumination of the few, which in no way makes up collective
transformation. And it is characteristic of the axial period that
the consciousness of the prophets goes unheard—just like the
"voice that clamors in the desert" that the Gospel of St. John
speaks of—and they themselves become converted into
victims by the destructive ignorance of the majority. Some of

the heroes of the axial period are crucified, in one way or another: Joseph is sold as a slave in Egypt, Socrates is condemned to death by hemlock, others retreat from the world—like Lao Tse, or Buddha who preached collective retreat. In any case, in our days we are dealing with a different consciousness than the one that in a previous era inspired the Holy War of the Aryans from ancient Iran or Vedic India: it is now about a consciousness that has shed grandiosity and lack of proportion characteristic of pharaohs or Greek heroes. We could say that, with the passing of the centuries, the dominant Aryans became impregnated by the matristic spirit of the peoples they dominated, and in India the spirit of the Upanishads was the fruit of this synthesis between the Vedic-Aryan world and the chthonic spirit of the more archaic cultures of Mohenjo-Daro and Harappa. The same thing occurs in the times of classical Greece during which Aeschylus in his Oresteia was explicit in his aspirations toward balance between the patriarchal spirit of his time and the matristic spirit of the past.

In the same way that the fruit of the axial period was consciousness for only a minority, the seed which would lead to later consciousness on a larger scale, the new consciousness that emerges at the beginning of the transformation of the individual can be said to be the seed of a future "illuminative phase" further down the road—since it is an insular consciousness that has not yet become integrated into the emotional world or the world of action. We could say that conversion or metanoia and enlightenment are different in the same way that the birth of an embryo is different from birth itself, or in the way that a seed is different from the tree that grows from it even when it hasn't yet given fruit. Analogically, the religions that sprung up in the axial period of history can be conceived as socio-cultural organisms of the seminal nature, and the seed of the Christian church does not seem to have given us yet a world in agreement with its ideals and precepts. The state of our collective consciousness, even in our apocalyptic times, is one in which the idea of a society ruled by wisdom and love continues to be a dream, a dream that perhaps most intellectuals consider incompatible with "human nature."

Just as the midlife crisis in which an individual goes through a transformation that is only partial - and that has more to do with the individual's mind than with his or her heart or body—after the catastrophe of the mythical "Iron Age" came into existence a spiritually superior subculture that only by staying away from the socio-cultural and political system or by being able to adapt to it was tolerated—and even highly respected. In light of the centuries, however, the price the old religions paid to be left alone becomes evident. In the case of Christianity this price is summed up in the famous saying "render unto Caesar what is Caesar's."

After the phase in which the path is begun and the period of aspiring and effort designated in Christianity as the "via purgativa" comes, in individual development, a new qualitative transition known as the "via illuminativa." It is then when what we could truly call spiritual life begins for the individual, since the individual is no longer only a seeker, but someone whose mind has been opened to the contemplative experience. Just like puberty, the doorway into maturity and into the path of life is a way to a new level of existence which could be spoken of in terms of a new birth. This transition is also the gateway to that phase of development in which the individual is captured by a spontaneous and irreversible evolutionary impulse.

Something similar can be said about the period in history called the European Renaissance. Just as individual life flourishes in the illuminative experience, we can say that our civilization flourished in the Renaissance, which was a true birth—since only then was there truly a synthesis between the Greco-Roman heritage and the Judeo-Christian heritage. More than anything else, however, the Renaissance was the beginning of the liberation through which the age-old secular and ecclesiastical authoritarianism was surpassed. And this liberation gave way to an acceleration in the rhythm of social evolution, seen in successive waves.

At the beginning the Renaissance was characterized by an affirmation of individual freedom that was principally expressed in the affirmation of the values that came from the Greco-Roman culture, eclipsed by centuries of medieval Christianity; after which the questioning of ecclesiastic authority became even more evident and gave way both to the corresponding strengthening of the power of the nobility and to the investigation of the world through observation and reason, relatively free from dogmatic thought.

Social revolutions followed, in France and in the European colonies in the Americas, during the time that we call "the century of light"—that not only held the triumph of reason of Kant and Voltaire, but also was the time in which Beethoven and Rousseau spoke out for liberation of the heart, giving origin to the romantic movement.

And once again the revolutionary wave characterized the next century, when scientific contributions became complicated with economic and human problems during industrialism. The revolutionaries of this time can be seen as implicit defenders of instinctualism, and the influence of Nietzsche, with his attack on Christian civilization in the name of life and the Dionysian spirit went so much further than anything commonly registered in the history of our culture when he was proclaimed the father of existential philosophy. The way in which he showed the real face of the unconscious hypocrisy of his contemporaries had no precedent, and it is understandable that Freud would say of Nietzsche that he had been the man who best knew himself. It was from him mainly that Freud inherited his own vision of "the vicissitudes of the instincts" under the empire of morality, and even though he did not go as far in his theoretical proposal as the condemnation of civilization (preferring, faced with the clear realization of its incompatibility with instinctive life, to condemn the latter) his practical work was that of the liberator of sexuality.

And what Freud did for sex, Marx did for hunger— meaning the needs associated with the instinct of conservation.

I suspect that, as a fractal structure, the entire historical process—observable through millennia—is analogically reflected in the structure of each of the civilizations in the way that certain parts of the structure that are shown on a detailed map are similar to the ones that can be seen on a larger scale. If we specifically consider the structure of Western civilization, at least, the analogy is clear. If we identify the time of birth with the birth of Christ, the Renaissance is similar to puberty, the Century of Light is the age of majority, and the era of Marx and Freud—which constituted a change in direction when faced with the consciousness of exploitation (social) and repression (psychic)—is the collective equivalent of a middle-age crisis.

According to this "microscopic" analysis of our specific historical cycle, the last wave of liberation—which would correspond to the illuminative phase in individual development—was that brief powerful planetary Renaissance of the 60s; a movement with characteristics at the same time neo-Freudian (because of its obvious therapeutic component) and neo-Marxist (because of its liberating spirit) which has been alluded to using expressions such as "the New Age" and "the Revolution of Consciousness." In this wider perspective that I propose, nevertheless, the cultural revolution of the "New Age" appears only to be a last phase—with planetary scope—in an illuminative and freeing process of social transformation that began in Florence during the 14th century.

In one way or another, the illuminative phase of development follows the "dark night of the soul," and if the isomorphism that I propose between individual and social levels is valid, it would be logical to expect a collective darkening of the conscience. Both the interpretation of the Renaissance as an illuminative phase in history and that of the cultural movement of the 60s as an illuminative phase in Western Christian civilization tell us that we are on the brink of the historical equivalent of that phase of "night" or "contraction." And in effect: in spite of all the technical progress it would seem that the process of liberation begun in the Renaissance had stopped a couple of decades ago.

But before we go on to consider the "dark night of the soul" as a paradigm for the critical times we live in, it would be good to stop to more closely examine the cultural wave of the 60s, as well as what the experience of individual development tells us about the transition between expansion (illuminative) of the conscience and the contraction that follows it.

I'll begin with the so-called "New Age," which at the time was considered by many to be the gateway to a happy world and that today appears to popular consciousness as a transitory Bohemian fad that has been overcome. It was about this time in history that Marilyn Ferguson wrote in her popular book *The Aquarian Conspiracy* of an allusion to the age of Aquarius (that according to astrologers follows the age of Pisces for the next 2000 and some years) as well as the expression "new age" that have suggested a way of seeing and feeling things that is closely related to a new therapeutic and spiritual culture that became manifest through a creative effervescence seen in the appearance of numerous schools and charismatic leaders, some with characteristics that justified Jacob Needleman—in his classic book about that time— referring to new religions.

But this therapeutic and spiritual movement took place in the larger context. It coincided—in times of the Vietnam War—with the awakening of pacifism and diverse movements that had to do with social justice, feminism, and ecology. This period of our cultural history was mainly defined by that which the historian Theodore Roszak, writing at the end of the 60s, described as the birth of a "counter-culture": a minority but notable subpopulation composed of individuals spurred by the knowledge that the "system" that we live in (the established system which at that time was called the "establishment") did not deserve our trust or our respect.

The awareness that "the world is crazy" has been generalized so much today that we forget it's a rather recent idea. Even though it was mostly clear to the thinkers of ancient spiritual traditions that the world lives "in sin" or in a type of carousel of dreams, the idea of a fall or degradation of the collective consciousness from a condition of greater spiritual plenitude that declined was forgotten and ended up being replaced—after Darwin and industrialism—by the belief in continual progress. It is to Freud that we owe the notion of the universality of neurosis, and it was surely the post-Freudians—like Fromm and his colleagues from the school of Frankfurt, as well as R.D. Laing and the group of humanist psychologists—who managed to understand it more completely. But in the decade of the 60s, the feeling that "the world is upside down" became popular and found a home mainly in people, generally young people, who, explicitly or implicitly disappointed in the conventional world, its values and its traditions, set out to search for new consciousness and life. They called themselves "hippies," but essentially they were young people who, unsatisfied with known paths, set out to leave the familiar behind to freely experiment with the unknown.

Today the word "hippie" has become associated with drug addiction and a problematic marginality, since the bourgeois counterrevolution that followed the "New Age" has conspired to successfully discredit it. Sasaki Roshi—a Zen master whom I heard give a conference in University of California in 1965—seems to have understood this prophetically. With implicit humor and certain provocation, he announced that he would speak on the spirit of Buddhism and proceeded to explain that it was the same as the hippie spirit. Buddha himself had become a hippie, explained Sasaki, when he left his parents' house with all its palatial comforts to go out in search for the truth.

But today the search for meaning that sustained that generation, has been criticized and even criminalized by the police spirit of a system that doesn't pass up an opportunity to attack the dangerous rebels, pointing out psychedelic enthusiasm. Invoking the defense of public health and sympathy for worried families, the Establishment criminalized drugs in a persecution only comparable with the prior war against the supposed dangers of communism. Through such persecution not only have jails been filled and the problems of youth squelched, but, suddenly, the sense of an emerging culture has been smashed under the stone of the ultra-respectable and repressive "Christian Right."

Just as for the individual the illuminative phase of development of the conscience is only a type of spiritual "honeymoon" during which the ego has only apparently disappeared without truly having been overcome, our spring-like "New Age" was somewhat like jumping toward the stars, and although it allowed some to identify a prophetic preview of a possible future, there is no doubt that those who thought we were at the gates of heaven were dreamers who were somewhat too optimistic. And after all this our current collective condition can be compared to the condition of Percival who, after having lost sight of the Castle of Mystery, had to face difficult tests in order to recover it. And after our collective honeymoon we find ourselves in a crisis so deep that we now ask ourselves if our apparent liberation was not just a dream or if what was conceived at that time will not end up aborted.

It is clearly apparent that the cultural wave of our time went through an expansive phase that began at the end of the 50s and a counter-revolutionary contraction phase that began to dominate at the beginning of the 80s, but one must remember that, in the individual and in the collective, apparent highs and lows cover a more complex reality: when it seems that we are progressing we are simultaneously falling, and when decadence is most notorious we will surely be able to see, in its interior, new development. And that is how, since the Renaissance, progressive liberation has been taking place along with simultaneous corruption and despiritualization. The apparent contradiction can be understood if we keep in mind that for each step in our development (both interior and social) a pathology develops inside of us that could be called parasitic: a personal or collective ego (which each of us carries) that feeds on our energy in order to form a dreamlike state that does not coincide with our needs or potential. And in the same way that during the individual "dark night" the pilgrim discovers that all his progress has been for naught—

since it has not brought the expected spiritual realization in physical life or in concrete interpersonal reality—so, it seems to me, that in our collective night we discover that we are still prisoners of the patriarchal pattern that is thousands of years old, and that has become more powerful than ever as technology progresses and as the order established through the empire of economic power is strengthened.

And, nevertheless, since it is only through transcending this collective "old man" that our progress can be in function of true evolution, we cannot ignore the opportunity that is inherent in our crisis.

It seems to me that we can apply to the process of collective transition that spans the 60s into the 80s the same information that we know about individual transition from the "illuminative phase" to the "dark night of the soul." After breaking into spiritual consciousness, the individual is overtaken by a process of enthusiastic inflation—the hybris that the ancient ones at times have called the "syndrome of the witch's apprentice," in which the insights of the spirit are applied in service to the ego—and this contributes to confusing the egotistical with the visionary, causing a later invalidation and repression of the new consciousness.

When, after his access to spiritual arrogance, the individual realizes that he has placed the grace received in service of his narcissism, his thirst for power or personal convenience, he sees himself as similar to Oedipus Rex when, looking upon his excesses and more, he tears his eyes out and condemns himself to exile. In the same way that an apprentice in spiritual life who begins to mature, having realized his arrogant excesses repudiates them, and begins his "night journey," so the inspiration of a subculture of young seekers was converted into a marketplace of charlatans and a "new narcissism," after which the profusion of false gold helped to make it so that the world could not recognize true gold. And that is the moment in which the New Age (in 1976) burned its hippie in effigy (in Golden Gate Park in San Francisco), able to see both the degeneration of its ideals and its defeat at the hands of the established order. In music, which so faithfully reflects the spirit of the times, the soft rock of the Beatles gave way to heavy metal, and the spirit of the "flower children" was replaced by the punks. The consciousness of youth groups went from hope to cynicism, and the internal child of each one, that had begun to suspect its intrinsic divinity, again became the evil one it had always been.

And that is how the counterculture—particularly in the environment of California students—after having inspired civil liberties movements, pacifism, feminism, ecology, and spiritual and therapeutic alternatives, seemed to fade away to such a degree that in our conservative times not only is Marx devalued and the spirit of the counterculture ridiculed, but it even seems to be out of style in modern life and its canons of good taste even to speak of the global capitalist empire that is destroying life on earth in the name of democracy and progress. Mass media is its faithful servant, and under its influence are governments and universities, all which allow totalitarianism, like the wolf in a fable, to effectively disguise itself as democratic sheep. Even philosophy, in its attempt to build a science of truth, contributes to the confusion through postmodern formulations. In the world of relativism that is promoted today everything is "un-buildable" and at the same time there is the declaration that all cultures (beginning with ours!) deserve respect. But the world works as if the only thing that could move it were money. And the only ideology sanctioned by political authorities in the contemporary world is the one that gives businesses the right to buy and sell freely in markets—which translates into the right to world-wide invasion of traditional cultures by the global capitalist empires and the priority of economic considerations.

Ever since the 80s the spirit of culture passed from the Bohemian to the bourgeois, from the romantic to the rational and practical, from antiauthoritarian to authoritarianism, from the anti-conventional to the "neoconservative," from the libertarian to a police state and from new age spiritual orientation to the Apogee of the Christian right wing that is like a contemporary echo of the attitude of Hernando Cortez and other Christian conquistadors, in whom the pretension of religious superiority and repressive morality serve the purpose of business and greed.

While during the 70s there was a spring-like climate of a newborn culture in California, during the last decades the climate has turned autumn-like, and what is most notorious are the signs of a dying culture as announced in the title of the voluminous book by the French historian, Barzun, *From Dawn to Decadence*, which deals with the 500 years that have passed since the Renaissance, as well as the more recent volume by Morris Berman that is about the United States, *The Twilight of American Culture*. But just as the "nighttime navigation" in the evolution of the individual is, in the best of cases, only the prelude to this stage that Christian mystical theology has named the "via unitiva," we can expect that our difficult times hold the potential for our plenitude as a species. Many have felt this, surely, and someone during the 70s specifically dealt with this topic in a book called *The Promise of the Coming Dark Age* in which the author developed the analogy of our times with the decadence of the Roman Empire. The counterculture of the seekers seems to have disappeared when faced with the implicit "killing of the innocent" which takes place in the apogee of the new neoliberal capitalism[1], and, even though the public was not aware of it, thousands of hippies ended up in jail, and it can also be said that the Bohemian and libertarian spirit of the

---

[1] As explained in the introduction to Chomsky's book *Profit over People*, "Neoliberalism is the defining political economic paradigm of our times. It refers to public politics and processes through which a few private interests control life and society as much as possible in order to maximize their own gain. Originally associated with Reagan and Thatcher, neoliberalism during the last two decades has been the dominant global political economic tendency adopted by center wing political parties and by many from the traditional left as well as those from the right. These parties and the politics they implement represent the interests of extremely wealthy investors in less than 1000 giant corporations."

"consciousness revolution" has penetrated the system and maintains vitality from inside its fissures.

Except among some academics and businessmen, the term neoliberalism is not very well known by the public, especially in the United States. There, on the contrary, neoliberal initiatives are called free market politics and are said to stimulate freedom of movement for private enterprise and consumers, to reward personal responsibility and business initiatives and to be against incompetent government and bureaucratic interference... a generation of efforts in public relations financed by corporations have given these terms and ideas an almost sacred-like air."

Theodore Roszak, historian to whom we owe the early chronicles of the counterculture, has recently published a book called *The Wisening of America* in which he observes that the demographic explosion in the U.S. called the *baby boom generation* has been combined today with longer life expectancies as a consequence of progress in medicine and that the result of both is a population never before seen of wise retired people: people with more emotional maturity than in other generations in whom not only survives the open spirit of the New Age but also the fruit of a long maturing period.

The analysis that Roszak makes of objective facts coincides with my conviction that the antidote to our presently extreme mercantile technocratic era is to be found in the spirit of our brief era of seeking. And it coincides with the vision that I proposed about 15 years ago in *The Agony of the Patriarchy*, which names the "new shamans" as vital yeast for our future. If the obsolescent aspect of our critical times is the patriarchal structure of society, its underdeveloped aspects are love and freedom—common factors in the world of therapy and genuine spirituality, at the same time notorious ideals of those young dreamers that today we remember with a certain learned despise..I would like to end with a quote from the last chapter of the book I just mentioned ("New Shamanism for Thousand-year-old Problems"):

So then, when I mention the new Shamanism, I'm not speaking about the same thing as those who believe that Shamanism is indissolubly connected with drums, feathers and totem animals. The type of Shamanism that is extending itself among us is certainly connected with this kind of influence because of a natural resonance with it (in the form of receptivity), but we should not forget that before this Shamanism had its origins in an autochthonous form and that only because of the sympathetic link between the emerging Shamanism and the old Shamanism are we interested in it now.

Finally, I believe that, especially in our times—when so many witches' apprentices are going through what I have called the "post-illuminative inflation syndrome" or the deep regression that this phase of descending into hell in the Shamanic journey implies—it makes sense to take a look at the fact that, no matter how much maturity the current generation lacks, it is to them, as pioneers in individual development, that most assuredly an important role in the process of collective transformation in which we are immersed will fall over time. In other words: in this population made up of seekers, somewhat marginal and mostly still only halfway through their journey, there lies a first-degree human resource with special meaning for this time of crisis; certainly the key to getting through it will not come from old institutions but from new fermentation.

I feel moved to use here a metaphor known for some time now in relation to individual transformation: the butterfly. Only now, using it as a symbol of collective transformation, it would have to be a macro-butterfly in which each of its cells would be the fruit of a butterfly-like blossoming in an individual who (through a kind of incubation and pilgrimage) has left behind, in his psychic journey, the original larva state.

I once heard Willis Harman say that a butterfly's metamorphosis implied, during its incubation in the chrysalis, that at the same time that old cellular structures were being disintegrated, a new central structure was being formed from cells that—because of the fact that it controlled the formation of the future organism, as if it held the code beforehand—received the name "imaginal."

Just as "imaginal" cells in the butterfly predicted the transformation of the larval body into a winged adult body, so we could also conceive the current pioneers of individual transformation as the "imaginal" cells of the future collective organism, the new emerging humanity.

If our crisis is moving us toward a future "Judgment Day," we will surely come to understand that we cannot serve the God of love and the God of money at the same time; but we should expect that only imminent fatality will allow us to stop our free fall into the abyss on time, and I hope that the proposed "night of the soul" as a paradigm of our critical times produces hope in the same way that *The Dark Night of the Soul* by St. John of the Cross gave candidates hope centuries ago. St. John of the Cross said that the soul in this phase of pilgrimage no longer needs to be chastised as it did in the phase of purification, which came before the enlightened period, for it is now God himself that chastises it, and the only answer is to keep the faith.

The Sufis, who have described very well how the phase of expansion of consciousness is followed by another of contraction, say that the latter is not a lesser blessing than the prior. This means that, in spite of the darkening of spiritual consciousness that this contraction holds, the experience of feeling a distance from the divine and of wishing for a "homecoming" is of immense value. It could be said that we need to feel impoverished in order to complete our development—just as a baby needs to interrupt breast-feeding and become interested in foods that correspond to greater maturity.

In his allegory of the inner journey, the Persian mystic, Attar, describes seven valleys that the individual must cross before coming into plenitude. Among the first are the phases of the illuminative stage: the valleys of seeking, of love, of knowledge, and of detachment. Continuing on the road, however, there is more pain and less enthusiasm, and travelers

must finally go through the valley of poverty and of
nothingness before meeting with the legendary king, in the
same way that the well-known story of the Exodus of the
Jewish people, with a psycho-spiritual relevance that goes far
beyond literal and historical interest, follows the episode of
the ascent to Mount Sinai and the long journey through the
desert and similarly evokes drought and scarcity.

Individual psycho-spiritual aridness and impoverishment are well-known together with a "death of the soul" that
coincides with the incubation of new life. On a collective
level, on the contrary, we still have not gone from autumn to
winter—no matter how strong we feel the spiritual
impoverishment of culture and can guess at the inevitable
impoverishment that our exaggerated exploitation of nature
holds for us. At times like these it is difficult not to see the
relevance of the ancient Biblical message about the Jewish
people walking through the desert: they are called to be
faithful to the revelation and to build an ark that will serve as a
mobile temple in their journey. In other words, they are asked
during their journey not to forget the vision of Sinai.
Translating this symbol to our cultural moment, the meaning
is even more specific than a simple call to connect with the
sacred, since the moment of revelation that we have not
heeded—our Sinai—has been none other than our brief and
quickly dismissed "revolution of the consciousness."

The prophets of the Old Testament lamented the
hardships of the people of Israel when they insisted on
conducts contrary to their alliance with God. In our age of
abundant information, it's difficult to contemplate recent
history without some surprise at the resistance there is to
learning. Not only was the victimization of the pioneers from
the axial time insufficient: not even genocide seems to be
lesson enough to push us into a common, fraternal and healthy
life. Just like the patient who goes to his therapist again and
again to reassure himself of what he has to do and yet keeps
putting it off, we continue to want to better understand what is
happening to us when wise men 2000 years ago explained it to
us quite clearly. Did Plato not lucidly demonstrate the need for

a wise government and the impossibility of separating the task of governing with educating in virtue? Our knowledge becomes more and more processed as our resistance generates ever more dense smoke curtains. How much pain will we need in order to wake up? How close to the abyss do we have to go before we completely understand that our patriarchal system—with its authoritarianism disguised as democracy, its violence disguised as good intentions, its exploitation, its persecution of luxury, and so on—is a ship that we would do well to abandon before it sinks?

## 2. The Road to a Healthy Society

*Do not cry for the dead, but for the apathetic masses of*
*cowards and weaklings who perceive the suffering and*
*injustice in the world and do not dare to speak.*

Ralph Chaplin

*Freedom is the path*

*on which duty treads.*

*Out with business and money*

*that enslave children and women!*

Totila Albert

### Getting to the Point

There is an expression in English that says, "Take care of
your pennies and the pounds will take care of themselves."
And that's also what common sense says: always take care of
details and concrete points.

Yet I think that common sense, with its lack of
subtlety, is wrong. I believe it is true, however, that, as the
gospel reads, it is good for us to give priority to *the kingdom
of heaven*, and trust that details will take care of themselves.

If the uncountable problems that weigh heavily on our
collective lives are only slightly remediable and since an
isolated solution does not necessarily bring us any closer to
improving our situation in general, it becomes urgent for us to
be interested in and face our goal-problem as soon as possible.

In the previous chapter I've outlined the proposition
that the root of our specific and concrete problems is found in
the patriarchal condition of our minds and our society, and that
this lack of order in intra- and interpersonal relationships
expresses a pathology in the way we love.

Before going on to consider what we can do to remedy
this situation, I wish—as a footnote to the preceding

paragraph—to repeat what I've said on other occasions about the patriarchal mind and its relationship to love.

### *Diagnostics*

A type of insanity seems to be inspiring the path human matters are taking. It's something that becomes more apparent every day and which many people have written about, giving diverse diagnoses. Many (Gabriel Marcel and Barbara Garson[1], among others) think that the worst of our evils is technocracy, or "technocratic totalitarianism," as Theodore Roszak prefers to call it. Willis Harman, in his book *An Incomplete Guide to the Future*, suggests that it all has to do with the mentality of industrialized man. He points out that beyond technology and the economic machinery of modern capitalism, the way of life that is derived from them implies a certain mentality, and that this is where we would have to look for the cause of all those consequences that, in spite of all of the good intentions, seems so difficult to find. Recently Capra, in his book *The Crucial Point*, proposes that more important even than an industrialized nation and the way of life that it brings, is the unilateral rationalism from which we have been looking at the world and ourselves.

At the end of the last century, Nietzsche had already pointed out the serious limitations in rationalism, and more recently the topic reappears frequently, in general ending up putting the blame on Descartes and Aristotle, which to me seems unfair. Aristotle was an initiate in the mysteries, and Descartes, besides having left us analytical geometry as an inheritance, was a man who was profoundly intuitive and religious. It seems ironic that beings such as these, so "nonlinear," would end up being thought of as the main representatives of the limitations of linear thought. All in all, it's still important that we recognize and question the fact that we've been managing the world and our own issues by the light of reason only.

In spite of the great importance this topic has in showing the need for mental change, I doubt that considering

that the super-rational mentality is the supporting column that
has given way to the current technological era has identified
the root of the problem. I tend to think that the excessively
rational cut of this diagnosis is rather suspicious—since it
seems to imply a unidirectional interpretation for emotional
attitudes (like ambition and authoritarianism) and political
evils (like nationalism and the hypertrophy of bureaucracy),
which are being considered mere complications derived from
a mistaken way of thinking.

It is of course true that knowledge influences the way
we feel, and that the religious, philosophical and mythical
view of the world, far from having been only a source of
positive liberation and transformation for humanity, has also
served to justify and cover up pathological attitudes and
behaviors. We could justify as well the consideration of
rationalism as the fruit of the will to dominate the world
through technology and as an expression of an attitude that is
excessively manipulative and greedy. Anti-spiritual scientific
thought and the tyranny of linear thought can be considered to
freeze knowledge in its analytical-utilitarian facet, and this, in
turn, suggests an anxious fixation on survival, sacrificing the
sacred rest needed for contemplation. I would say that
anxiety—Maslow's "motivation that comes from deficiency,"
or Freud's pre-genital libido (oral or anal)—exist
interdependently with the Cartesian vice that is part of the
technological age.

I think, nevertheless, that it is valid to aspire to provide
a unified explanation of our cognitive, emotional and
sociopolitical diseases, and in this spirit I want to suggest the
idea that the "patriarchy" is the common root of the industrial
mentality, of capitalism, of exploitation, of alienation, of the
incapability to live in peace, of the exploitation of the earth,
and of other evils that we suffer from.

I could limit myself to saying (as I have throughout the
years) that the source of all the evils in our society and what
has brought us to this current crisis is our limited capacity for
healthy human relations. Surely no one will argue if I say that
it is our limited capability to love—or, if you prefer, our

incapability to obey the Christian command to love our neighbor as ourselves—that keeps us from having relationships that are truly fraternal with those around us, and it would seem that it would be enough to recognize that the limitation of our loving capacity generates a society that is ill and that manifests a legion of secondary problems. But we could be more precise yet in our diagnosis if we concentrate more exactly on what it is that comes between us and our capability for brotherhood: the word "patriarchal" invites us to think that the reason we fail to create fraternal relationships among ourselves, along with the reason we become incapable of authentically loving ourselves (in that way denying ourselves the natural loving flow toward others) is the persistence of obsolete links with authority and dependence which are the seat of tyranny of the paternal over the maternal and the filial.

To say that our disease resides in the "patriarchy" is the same as saying that the problem is as old as civilization itself, and that to get out of the hole we've dug we have to question everything that we've done since almost forever; change structures so deeply seated that it's difficult for us to differentiate the essential nature of being human from our current manifestation, a product of conditioning.

The topic of the patriarchy was introduced by the Swiss philosopher Johan Jacob Bachofen (1815-1887), who cultivated the philosophy of history and social philosophy and whose work on the matriarchal regime in the original European religion had great influence on later anthropologists as well as on the feminine movement, on Nietzsche, on Engels, and on other authors.

It is surprising that Bachofen was capable of discovering the preexistence of a world centered on the mother figure that came before patriarchal civilizations and that we are now familiar with through information as disperse it is scarce, like for example information on customs of diverse ancient peoples transmitted by Herodotus and Thucydides. Using a notable combination of intuition and erudition, he was able to formulate a theory of social evolution that, according to his conclusions, had seen three statuses. The first phase ("telluric/geological") would have been composed of promiscuity and maternity without marriage; then, as a reaction to this phase would have come a second "lunar" phase, in which marriage would have been instituted as a regulating principle and in which women would have taken exclusive property of children and land—this phase would coincide with the forming of communities in stable territory and the birth of agriculture—and a final "solar" phase, the patriarchy, that would have consecrated paternal conjugal rights, the division of labor, individual property and the institution of the State.

Joseph Campbell, in his introduction to the English translation of *Myth, Religion and Maternal Rights*, says that in order to study mythology as Bachofen did it was necessary "to leave behind the conditioned way of thinking and living of the time," and goes on to cite a commentary made by Bachofen to his teacher (in an autobiographic piece written as a requirement): "Without a complete transformation of the being, without recovering ancient simplicity and health for the soul, it is impossible to reach even the most minimum level of the greatness that the ancient times enjoyed, nor the way of thinking of those days in which the human race had not strayed from, as it has today, harmony with creation and the transcendent Creator."

As a teacher of the psychology of archetypes before the word was even invented (he called them "Grundgedanken": "fundamental thought"), Bachofen exercised profound influence on Joseph Campbell, who, with all the elegance of his own rank as University professor, would level a solid blow against patriarchy by ironically presenting the zealotry centered on the father figure found in the middle east within the universal context of religions in the mythology of the entire world. Since I don't have the slightest doubt that Joseph Campbell gave us a decisive backdrop for the inspiration of the goddess-based religion, popular today within the feminist movement, I believe it is appropriate to consider Bachofen the cultural grandfather of the same.

The influence of Bachofen on anthropology was enormous, in spite of the fact that today that influence is barely visible. Having given powerful impulse to this science, then newly born, his ideas quickly became considered outdated.

But after Morgan and others, inspired by Bachofen, had stimulated an entire generation of anthropologists to question cultural evolution, the proof of the existence of a contemporary "matriarchy" became unclear and the anthropological confirmation of Bachofen's historical view became questionable. Perhaps this is why anthropology became less and less interested in compared studies and became inclined more toward trying to understand cultural characteristics within the significant context of the concrete society in which they appeared.

Certainly anthropology (and, within its scope, particularly Malinowski and Margaret Mead) has shown us many non-patriarchal societies that still exist, but we don't know to what degree the knowledge of these societies brings us closer to truly understanding prehistorical societies. The most notable summary of what was known about peoples and cultures in which the mother figure prevailed, when the topic began to lose interest for specialists, can be found in the monumental work by Robert Briffault, *The Mothers*, published in 1927. It was written to counteract the prevalent idea that patriarchal institution was an expression of natural law, and in this sense it was well received. To him we also owe the displacement of attention placed on the authority of the mother to the inheritance through the maternal lineage and the question of whether a wife should reside after marriage in the home of the husband or vice versa. He was also the first to present the idea that marriage was originally a group contract, in which a man belonging to one of the groups would have sexual access to any woman from another group or groups, at the same time being denied access to the women of his own group.

Even more meaningful than anthropological discoveries has been the fact that Bachofen's affirmations were confirmed by archaeological discoveries in the Middle East and in ancient pre-Aryan Europe, especially in connection with the agricultural revolution that took place during the Neolithic era. In these digs were found literally thousands of female figures (baptized on occasions as Venus), pregnant women whose arms and feet are barely present, and which seem to be basically bellies, in which even the heads were no more than a simple vortex on a type of triangle formed by the body. The iconographic aspect seems representative of the capacity of nature to procreate, and throughout Europe there seems to have been a far-reaching religious sentiment in relation to a female deity, a deity that was creative, procreative, and related to fertility. Marija Giambutas has done extensive in research into this topic.

Also in what today is known as Turkey, cities have been uncovered that date back to 6000 BC, in which, unlike what happened in later patriarchal cities, there are no signs that revealed the existence of war for a period that lasted 15 centuries before these cities were destroyed by Indo-European migrations.

The following historical era is today well known to us. The Indo-European people were the patriarchal conquerors who, in virtue of the supremacy they acquired through the use of two concrete techniques—the domestication of the horse and the metallurgy of iron—were able to submit the matristic cultures (to use the expression devised by Giambutas in reference to the cultural domination of feminine values, and not by the supposed authority of women as the term "matriarchal" would imply).

Nevertheless, it is not in the specialized field of archaeology or in the field of ethnology where the word "patriarchal" became best known. There is no doubt his word is intimately associated with the feminist movement. Even though patriarchy, through all it represents, makes up the archetypal enemy of humanity from its very roots, at the beginning it only seemed to represent a threat to the world of women. So, the book by Eve Figes, *Patriarchal Attitudes*, written in the first decades of our century, is effectively a plea against masculine injustice. It is a political work that compares sexist chauvinism with anti-Semitism and hoists the flag of defense of the oppressed and exploited.

Only later was it shown that the archetypal enemy of women also deserved to be considered the enemy of children and, since we all have some child in us, the enemy of all. I have found in Mary Daly's book, *Gyn Ecology*, a reference to the work by François Enbonne, *Le Féminisme ou la Mort*, in the form of the phrase "eco-feminism." She sustains that "the destiny of the human race and the planet is at risk and no revolution headed by men will be capable of counteracting the horrors of overpopulation and the destruction of natural resources." Mary Daly continued her reflection in an essay on the "meta-ethics of radical feminism" by writing, "I share this basic premise, but the focus and accent are different. Although I'm worried about all forms of pollution generated by a phallocratic society, this book is more about mental-spiritual-bodily pollution derived from patriarchal myth and language in all levels. These levels go from determined grammatical styles to the handling of what's attractive, from religious myth to off-color jokes, from theological themes that celebrate the 'real presence' of Christ in the sacred host to the commercial that announces the 'sensation of living' that Coca-Cola gives, or the falsified label on canned products. Phallic myth and language generate, legitimize and mask over material contamination that threatens all life forms on this planet."

Mary Daly sustains that the seven capital sins in which the holy fathers of the church sum up the evil of human nature have been a product of phallocracy (the names she gives the patriarchal aberration of society).

Riane Eisler, nevertheless, has even more explicitly accused the patriarchy of being the essential problem of humanity. By reformulating fundamental information found in specialized research, Eisler reminds us that the patriarchy, far from forming part of the nature of humanity, was the result of a fall from the pre-patriarchal paradise-like condition of the Neolithic era. This author, in her book *The Chalice and the Sword*, presents to us the idea that to speak of "patriarchal order" is equivalent to speaking of a world in which dominance is based on masculine predominance through power, and that we should see in this the fundamental aberration of our culture. The importance of this idea alone gives this book a much greater weight than that of a simple work of historical and anthropological information, sufficiently perhaps to justify Ashley Montagu's saying that he had never recommended a book more, since it "deserves to be considered as the most important work since Darwin's *The Origin of the Species.*"

I did not, however, take from Eisler the idea that patriarchy is the essence of our macro-problem. My interest in this topic dates back to the middle of the 50s and the source of my inspiration is somewhat older and less known yet: a Chilean artist and visionary, Totila Albert—who was at that time already conscious of how critical our situation was. But before saying more about his vision I would like to share my most recent explanation of our "inner beings," which seem to me to correspond to our three brains and that express themselves in different ways of loving. For this I'm going to insert what was said in "The Love Convention" celebrated in the Gestalt Institute of Barcelona some years ago.

### *Of Good Love and the Other Kind*[1]

I would like to begin by celebrating the initiative of the organizers of this event in inviting us all to an encounter on the topic of love and therapy. I think it is a topic that deserves all the attention it can get. Therapy has to do with a lot of things, so it is possible to talk about "therapy and this" or "therapy and that": therapy and understanding oneself, "therapy and that": therapy and understanding oneself, for example, or therapy and pain, therapy and transference, etc. The relationship between the topic of love and the topic of therapy is much more intrinsic. We could say that all

---

[1]Conference presented at The Love Convention, Barcelona, 2001

discomforts that are treated in therapy come from a problem of loving, that all emotional problems begin with the lack of love in the life of the person. Although today the word "neurosis" is disappearing, it seems to me that it has been useful as a reference to a common root in all emotional problems, and it is still true that the origin of the different neurosis - whether "symptomatic" or "character base"—is found in the difficulties with and problems with love. And therapy, in its processes, has a lot to do with love. It is not that love is enough—I don't believe it is—in order for therapy to be good; but even psychoanalysts today agree that insight is not the most important issue in psychoanalytical therapy (which has been so essentially oriented toward insight during its entire history), but that the relationship is. And when we talk about relationship we mean to state in a scientific fashion what so unscientifically would be called "love," or at least benevolence. And the objective of therapy is also love, or at least I think that I'm not the only person present who thinks that happiness comes through love and that if happiness is a characteristic of healthiness, it can be linked to the capacity to love and to the need to heal our own loving capacity.

Now, going into the specific topic "Of Good Love and the Other Kind," I suppose that anyone who lives in Spain or who is Spanish will recognize in this title a reference to Archpriest of Hita and to his book "The Book of Good Love." But I do not share the vision of the Archpriest when he said that only the love given to God is good. In that work, the love of God and carnal love are opposites. And the proposal that I would like to make here is that both are good loves, that they are two components of good love, since love is not just one thing. From a certain point of view we could say that there are many loves. Mendelssohn commented, when talking about musical language, that it is not less exact than verbal language, but that it is more specific because each joyful musical phrase expresses a different joy. In the same way, we could say that gestures of love are uncountable. We could say that there are people who love through their capacity to admire, people who love through their capacity for tolerance, people who love through their capacity for gratefulness: there are many manifestations of the emotion that has to do with love, but it seems to me that just as all space can be described using three coordinates, there are also three basic elements in what we call love, three fundamental loves.

One of these loves could be called Freudian love, eros—love that is intimately linked to sexuality and which for Freud was the basic love. For Freud friendship was erotic love deprived of its objective and benevolence was a transformation of eros. But it is so much easier and less complicated to think of benevolence as a love that is different from eros and which we could call Christian love. No matter what Freudians say I do not believe that to speak of "loving thy neighbor as thyself" has to do with sublimated erotic love. It would be more natural, it seems, that generosity and empathy exist in their own right, to say it in one way, and that is what Christianity has designated as charity, or, in Greek, agape. Intuitively we feel that sexual attraction does not normally come from a compassionate attitude; nor does compassion come from sexuality; we must therefore, speak of eros and agape, or of love and charity.

But there's also a third love, which seems so different to me than these other two, as much as these two are different between themselves, and this third love deserves to be looked at as relatively autonomous: this is the love that is implied in friendship and which we could call filial in keeping with the Greek terms we have been using here and in reference to the word used by Plato when referring to something much different than what today we call "platonic love"—which is a sublimated manifestation of the erotic impulse. In the love that we could more adequately call "Socratic," since even though Socrates used the word eros in reference to the love of an ideal—beauty, grandiosity, good and all other things that have intrinsic worth—this love for ideals or ideas is only by analogy comparable to the loving attraction between the sexes. Love for justice and love for the divine, in my opinion, are not only different from eros in their object, but also in their nature and subjective quality: while the erotic wakes the appetite, this third love, that underlies relationships that are not erotic or centered on help or protection but on "disinterested" friendships, takes into account value. We could call it love-adoration, but where common feelings are concerned its typical manifestation is appreciation. The three loves, then, are related to desire, kindness (that gives way to compassion) and appreciation (which sees itself exalted in admiration and gives way to adoration).

We could speak generally of eros as love-pleasure: a love that takes pleasure in another, that takes pleasure in the beauty of another, and going beyond a definition strictly linked to sexuality, we could include what Buddhists call *mudita*, which is happiness that comes from others' happiness, which is very different from compassion as shown in benevolence, which does not want to see the other suffer. (One has more to do with eros, the other with agape.)

We could think that kindness is the most human of the manifestations of love, but that would not be exact. Even though the greater or lesser generalization of benevolence is human, in its origins love-kindness was intimately linked to maternal love, as a natural extension of what a mother feels for their offspring (and I use the word "offspring" in preference to children in order to refer to something that is not exclusive of humans, but rather of all mammals).

Is then love of ideals more human than kindness itself? Sometimes we say that a kind person is very "human" because we speak of humanity as a synonym of benevolent love. And we associate love-adoration with fanatics and their many inhumane acts. At the moment I would only like to point out that appreciatory love also has biological roots and antecedents, since in the beginning this love of what is seen as great (which contrasts with the maternal love of that which is small) is very much like what a child feels for his father.

If the mother is the one who gives us what we need, satisfying our wishes, the father is the one she is contemplating, the one that the mother values. The mother, who gives us everything, is the original source of values, and

is also the original model with respect to what is of value—
and so it happens that the mother implicitly delegates the order
of values to the father, simply because the child perceives that
she loves him. It has to do then with agape, with the mother's
love, and love of ideals has something to do with father's love.
And I think it has a biological root, not only because it derives
from an archaic proto-psychological situation in our individual
lives, but also because valuing something is closely related to
imitation, which is not only in our origin as cultural animals,
but is also much more archaic than culture and language.
Think of how chicks follow the first object that moves close to
them—it could be the hen but could also be (as investigations
of the phenomenon of imprinting have shown) a shoebox. As
Lorenz observed decades ago in his experiments with ducks,
the animals were linked for life to the object in question, that
could've been as arbitrary as an alarm clock.

Although humans are immensely more complex than
ducks and chickens, which means that we can only speak of
imprinting metaphorically in our case, we also have an innate
disposition to follow a model, and in our adult life it is clear
that we allow ourselves to be guided by those we admire.
Haven't we all had the experience of falling into imitating the
speech of a person we admire? And we surely remember how,
as children, we admired the hero of a movie and came out of
the theater walking the way he did.

Imitation is a biological impulse that makes us human,
and by imitating sounds used by our parents we learned to
speak. And we don't only imitate individual characteristics in
our parents but we imitate everything that is generally admired
which is precisely how culture is transmitted.

A new science has come about lately, whose name has
not been defined yet, but I suppose it would be something like
memetics, by analogy with genetics—in which a point of view
was adopted that states that a hen is the means by which eggs
are perpetuated, and we are the means in which genes are
transmitted. This point of view, proposed by Dawkins in
biology, has inspired analogous thought with respect to
memes, which are cultural entities, like language. It proposes

then, that things happen as if ideas used humans to perpetuate themselves and transmit themselves through our reproductive capacity. It is an idea that is catching on, and various books have been written about the imitative capacity of humans that makes it possible for thoughts to survive and is so inseparable from our identity. Not only because imitation is human, but because imitation is part of everything we consider part of our humanity: we know that people raised among savages or animals are not only lacking language or culture in a sense frequently used as something extrinsic to nature itself, but as intrinsic aspects of what we consider to be human.

But I digress, and I would like to complete a thought that I interrupted: there is a love that has to do with the mother, a love of that has to do with the father and a love that has to do with the child. Love-desire is more characteristic of the child in the original triad. Love that bases itself on the satisfaction of one's own desires is the love that is with us from birth, and we could say that it is the child within us that continually seeks satisfaction and freedom.

Just as the famous Catalan—Raimundo Paniker—relates the three persons in the holy Trinity with the grammatical persons I, you, and he, we could say the same for the three loves. Love-desire is a love that centers on the "I." A mother's love is related to the "you." Transpersonal love—love of ideals or love of the divine—has to do with the relationship with the "he." Love-kindness, of the maternal type, that we share with all mammals (even though we are not all so good and generous) is clearly more emotional, while it is sometimes said that appreciatory love is too intellectual. If a man joins a woman because he considers her to be an excellent person, for example, he could be told that his love for that woman is too intellectual in the sense that heart seems to be missing. Erotic love, on the other hand, is much more instinctive.

It seems then that these three loves are related to our three brains. The instinctive brain relates to eros, the emotional or middle brain (which is the mammal brain) relates to agape, and a truly human brain or neocortex relates to appreciatory love which looks to the heavens (which is different from instinctive love which looks to the earth, or maternal love which looks to the offspring).

I already explained my understanding of the ingredients of good love. But let's take a look at what makes bad love.

Perhaps we can say that in the end it is all love, and in that way we would have to say that only good love and its deviations and perversions exist. I, for one, deeply feel the truth in the last line of the Divine Comedy which tells us about "the love that moves the sun and all other stars." In this way it makes sense to conceive love as the central force not only of all that is human but also of universal creation. When a newspaper man asked Einstein about the most important mystery of science, Einstein answered with the question, "Could it be that the Universe is good?"; meaning to consider if in creation there could be a benevolent intention or not. But in general scientists have been satisfied with asking less, and our current concept of science characterized by the exclusion of the questioning as to the why of things - the teleological aspect that any question about the "final cause" asked by those in ancient times referred to. So the concept of universal love marks the difference between merely scientific perception and aesthetic or poetic perception, or metaphysical or religious perception—anything that involves "the other side of the mind." But it is not necessary for us to go back to the idea of a possible cosmic love in order to ask ourselves about the evils in love, we know these first-hand.

First of all are the obstacles to love. And it is obvious that compassionate love is not compatible with hate. Rage closes hearts. And fear is antagonistic with respect to erotic love. If someone has felt threatened or punished for their desires (and we know since Freud how frequent the resulting castration fantasies are) they will not dare to seek pleasure. Appreciation for someone does not walk hand in hand with envy or with competition. But in general all passions interfere with all types of love. All neurotic needs interfere with love.

There are also false loves; the falsifications of love. Compassion could be characterized as a high level energy, one of the highest values (and when St. John says, "God is love," he surely referred to compassionate love, benevolent love), but a large part of what the world calls kindness is based on the superego—unresolved internalized cultural mandates that tell us "you should be good," implying mandatory compassion and the threat: "you must... if not you'll go to hell." And each individual implicitly condemns himself for not being good enough and effectively goes to hell in life. This is not a very loving attitude, and what we call compassion is infrequently more than the result of a good education and falseness.

Erotic love is also falsified. Just as there is healthy and true instinctive love, which is profoundly satisfactory, there is a false erotic love is used to buy love, a type of seduction in which sexuality is placed at the service of the hunger for protection, inclusion, or company. It is not the sexual instinct that drives a person in these cases, but neurotic needs like avoiding loneliness or insignificance—needs that disguise themselves behind the mask of eros.

And is not love-respect falsified in a similar way as benevolence is? The Mosaic commandment "honor thy father and thy mother" is based on the understanding that a healthy person feels natural admiration toward those who were the first "Gods" in his or her life. During our first childhood our parents, who were the example of what it was to be an adult, surely seemed as large to us then as the divine or supernatural seems to us as adults, and although perhaps we have forgotten, it is significant that our experience of the divine throughout history has been formulated mainly through the images we have of our parents. Even though we cannot ignore that sometimes parents are people who are emotionally ill and poorly equipped for their function, I believe there is great truth in the observation of Iamblichus (a follower of Pythagoras), as reiterated by Gurdjieff, that states that a good man loves his parents.

Nevertheless, and in spite of the truth that the fourth commandment holds, after centuries of authoritarianism, the imperative of loving our parents makes us more infantile. It is not true love that inspires social and family mandates, but servile love; and more generally, the homage that is paid to so many things—both to ideals and to people—as part of an obedient gesture.

I don't think it's necessary to demonstrate or explain the fact, evident in all of our personal experiences, that false loves also constitute interferences for real love. They make up a negative use of psychic energy comparable to what happens in the nutrition and the biological energy of an organism that is feeding a parasite. The individual who "loves" only by remaining blind to his self-deceit perpetuates his own lie and lack of consciousness—which then become obstacles for authentic life and love. On the contrary, when a person gets to know himself through a therapeutic or spiritual process, sooner or later he discovers that he doesn't truly love, and only after this discovery of the falsification and emptiness can he begin to discover real love. But a person has to be extremely virtuous in order to realize that he doesn't love, since our well-being derives mostly from feeling that we are loving people, and we invest a lot in giving the image of being good people. It's very difficult, even heroic, to shed this illusion and fall into the abyss which takes us mysteriously to true life and its values.

And there are loves that are eminently parasitic: ways of loving that are deficiencies disguised as love. Essentially they are ways to fill one's own emptiness, ways to compensate what we lack using someone else's love. And it seems to me that these parasitic loves can also be divided into three types, according to the type of love that their hunger pursues.

We surely all know people who suffer and lose themselves in an exaggerated search for love through emotional relationships or sexuality that are so closely related to the feeling of being accepted and valued. Even when it seems that we're looking more for pleasure than love, I think it might be an illusion that hides an unrecognized search for love through sex.

Other people (that have been more dependent on their mothers in general) look for protection. As children they lacked care and now they go through life as orphans or feeling unprotected, looking for the care they lacked and wishing to inspire compassion.

And there are people who above all seek respect, people who don't look for "love" in the more common sense of the word, but look for recognition or admiration—and they dedicate a great part of their life and energy to being important. This is what we commonly call "narcissism"—a passion that shows that we wish to be loved in this way: to be considered important, great, and superior.

And of course, the greater the parasitic love is, in other words the more energy the person needs to use to fuel his or her love-seeking machine, the more occupied he or she is in finding love, the less probable it is that he or she will find it. It's like pushing on a door that only opens from the inside. (Many times I've cited Kierkegaard's metaphor from one of his books that observes that the door to paradise only opens from the inside.) This is why we have to calm our passions, learn not to push so much, develop true receptiveness to what is.

If I ended my exposition here after having mentioned my considerations about bad loves and spoken about the ingredients of good love, it wouldn't surprise me if I left the impression that I haven't said anything new. Even though perhaps my inclusive attitude and the way that I ordered the ideas could boast a certain novelty, it doesn't seem to me that there is anything new in the repertoire of good and bad loves that I presented. But I'm not finished yet, and it seems to me that the newest idea that I can share with respect to love (and this is what I would like to examine more in a practical way in a workshop format) is the idea that health and also plenitude in a loving life are related closely to the balance between our three loves. This implies that perhaps we can advance toward a more complete form of loving through the analysis of our own "loving formula."

We all have a determined formula. Some have much more erotic love and less compassion, others have a high level of love for the divine—devotional love—and very little erotic love. It seems to me that the so-called Christian commandment (which in reality is not only Christian, since it is found in Deuteronomy and in the spirit of the ancient Jewish tradition) points directly to the harmonizing of the different loves.

Surely all those present remember the famous words of Christ when he said that the entire Law of Moses could be summed up as: "Love thy neighbor as thyself and love God above everything," but perhaps you haven't noticed the triple commandment included that makes allusion to the three good loves we talked about. In the first place, Jesus (reiterating a precept already found in Deuteronomy) exhorts us to love our neighbors (benevolent, compassionate or maternal love). In the second place, He takes an element of comparison which is the love for oneself, the love for one's own desires, inner creature, inner animal; a wish for happiness that is directed toward our instinctive self that is comparable to erotic love or a child's love. And lastly, Jesus names the love of God, which is obviously appreciatory love, which corresponds to a father's love, and which finds in sacredness its supreme expression as love-adoration.

I think the idea of examining the balance between our three loves, or perhaps the imbalance, could be fruitful. And surely taking on such an analysis would help us realize that when one of our loves fails or is underdeveloped, we try to compensate through an impossible search. In this way, a person could be loving God desperately to compensate for his difficulty in loving flesh and bone people, or a person could be desperately seeking plenitude through romantic love when what he most needs is to open up to devotion, aesthetic feelings or to the gratefulness that is found in transpersonal values. Later on I'll invite you to question imbalances and the attempts at compensation that only perpetuate the unsatisfactory situation, and also to ask yourselves what can be done to balance the three ingredients of a loving life.

I want to point out that this last idea is not mine either, I've adopted it from a fellow Chilean, the poet and sculptor Totila Albert, who many of you have heard me speak about and whose vision of history was the source for my book, *The Agony of the Patriarchy*. In that book I also talked about his vision of what he called "Three Times Ours," a world made possible by beings that have reached this internal balance between their internal mother, father, and child. It was this intra-psychic three-way embrace that he considered the essence of health and a condition found in complete beings. A person in whose heart father, mother, and child embrace each other with their respective loves, naturally will not succumb to the tyranny of the intellect, to imbalanced emotionalism, or to impulsive anarchy - and I believe that he was right in thinking that only through massive individual transformation can we aspire to find an alternative to the patriarchal society and its archaic vices.

I'd like to end then with this idea: true good love requires not only good ingredients, but a balanced formula. Naturally, each of the formulas for love is intimately related to a character type (which in turn is linked to a characteristic deficit) but besides using the transforming potential of the knowledge of our own personality, I think it behooves us to attend to how the expression of our loving potential is unbalanced, and based on what we observe find ways to reeducate ourselves—seeking out experiences, influences and tasks that can help us overcome our deficiencies.

## *The Promise*

I called the first chapter of this book "The Promise of a Dying Civilization" without actually reformulating this promise other than implicitly and predominantly negatively: that we can comprehend and transcend our collective patriarchal ego so that, upon completing our development, we are able to survive the flood or the desert that awaits us, and our progressive and collective "journey through the underworlds" may purify us as it makes us wiser in order to establish healthy relationships. In this way we could reach, in time of course, the spiritual plenitude that so many cultures have intuitively perceived and that we all yearn for: the "Kingdom of God" of the prophets, equivalent to "the kingdom of heaven" on Earth.

Besides formulating the hope that the lesson of history wakes us sufficiently for the next transition toward a human condition free from obsolete psycho-historical conditioning, I want to consider the hope for a post-patriarchal condition through the ideal proposed by Totila Albert that includes harmony among our psychobiological components: father, mother and child.

Known as a sculptor in his youth, first in Germany and then in Chile, Totila Albert began an inner journey that made him a "man of knowledge" who was able to leave behind a vast poetic work (in German). But more than the art in itself, in the years during which I knew him, he was interested in helping people understand the necessary destruction of the patriarchal world and the saving value of what he used to call "the message of the three."

From the personal experience of psychological death and spiritual rebirth—that for him came in the form of an Orphic journey spurred by the death of his father—Totila Albert was able to balance "his three" and hoped that his poetry would help others to have healthy intra-psychic and intra-family relationships.

We could say that the main focus of his life's work was the understanding of what we could call the "mystery of the Trinity," which, surpassing specifically Christian language, meant the capacity of contemplating everything in such a way that in each thing or process reality becomes manifest to us with two sides, and at the same time we come to understand that between the yins and yangs there is a third factor that is not negative or positive but that serves the function of reconciliation: a "power of nothingness."

Totila Albert saw our "three principle" in the structure of the embryo, made up of three "layers" (ectoderm, mesoderm and endoderm) just as in the structure of the family and also on the transpersonal or cosmic level—since we are "children of the heavens and the earth," material and mental beings potentially capable of identifying with the transcendental as well as with our "mother nature." Albert understood history as a series of steps in which we incurred in successive and inevitable imbalances—since our survival and evolution depended on it. The vision of history that Totila Albert had is implicit in the vision I presented in the previous chapter.  He imagined that in the most archaic phase of our collective evolution we lived through something that could be called Darwinian anarchy, during which the strongest and roughest were able to overcome the dangers of scarcity. According to Totila, this "barbarianism" of our remote nomadic ancestors, peoples who moved throughout the seasons of the year following the sun, was what mythology called the golden age.  He called it the "filiarchy" because of its emphasis on the values of youth (think of Eskimos who in their migrations abandoned the old and the weak on the route).

Also, the organization of society around feminine values (and, as a result, communitarian sentiment) was seen by Albert as a necessary imbalance, in contrast to those feminists who have wished to propose our matristic era as a type of paradise.  The patriarchal revolution happened for a reason, after all, when a new consciousness, which strived to be heard, opted for taking over power.  We now know how throughout ancient history, because of a certain curse of power, patriarchal domination became degenerated at the same time that it enthroned itself—until it became the current, apparently anonymous, authority in the hands of a few that hide behind the screen of marketing laws.

"We have not yet lived with our Three in harmony," Totila Albert used to say, while preferring to refer to what the prophets named "the kingdom of God" as "The Three Times Ours," meaning something akin to "our holy three-part reality"—in implicit reference to our traditional Our Father. During the years of military dictatorship in Chile, unfortunately, Totila Albert's seven-meter-long bas-relief was destroyed. It was on the façade of a boarding school founded by President Pedro Aguirre Cerda and depicted this idea and at the same time a visionary experience that he had at the beginning of his inner journey: it was the image of a condor in flight with the human family on its wings and under its claws: the father on the right wing pointing to the heavens, the mother on the left wing pointing down to the Earth, and the son held by the condor in its claws and pointing with his index finger straight ahead.

Only very slowly have I come to understand the importance of the formula proposed by Totila Albert of an ideal that not only contemplates plenitude and balance, but also the comprehension of these as a condition of the reciprocity of "love among three": and as the years pass it seems to me even more relevant to bring this desideratum of psychic and interpersonal life to therapists, educators and spiritual guides.

I have also come to see how right Totila was in his criticism of historic Christianity because of its complicity with the patriarchy—pointing only to the internal world of the individual and leaving the aberration of human relations in the family unattended.

It seems to me that the vision of a healthy social condition as the balance between the paternal, the maternal and the filial, goes much further than the politics of relationships—between sexes or generations—and I imagine that not only would it be inspiring for the therapeutic-spiritual area and for the philosophy of society, but also for education in the third millennium. I will end with some thoughts on how this vision could be understood in relation to a non-patriarchal concept of government.

### Three-brained Politics

Saying that the healthy society that we could aspire to includes an awakened humanity that is made up of conscious, balanced beings is important, but it tells us little about the alternative system—about the desirable transformation of our institutions.

In an effort to find out about what informed critics of the system are saying today about how we could live better, I have recently read David Korten's book on the topic that he has called *The Post-Enterprise World*, and have found that a large part of this book also proposes the optimization of individual consciousness and that only near the end of chapter thirteen does he talk about decisions that have to do with *modus vivendi*, and even then he begins with a quote from the theologian Mathew Fox that points out the primacy of spirituality, that, as we know, cannot come into the world if it is not through each of us. He says:

"Living and subsisting must not be separated, but must flow from the same source, which is the Spirit. Spirit means life, and life, as well as making a living, are involved in living deeply, meaningfully, purposefully, joyfully, and with the consciousness of contributing to the community."[2]

Korten then gives an account of the considerations of Alicia Gravitz, director of COOP America, an organism that is concerned with the good use of economic power. Her vision of a healthy and desirable life can be summed up in the following considerations:

- A secure means of subsistence that can cover our basic material needs and give us respect in the community.
- A supportive family, friends, and a pacific, safe community that allows us to explore and develop our capabilities for establishing loving relationships.
- The opportunity to learn and to express the consciousness of ourselves and of the world that surrounds us, intellectually and artistically.
- Good physical health and the opportunity to participate in athletics, in dance and in other activities that allow us to feel how our energy vibrates in our bodies.

---

[2]Matthew Fox *The Reinvention of Work: A New Vision of Livelihood for our Time* (San Francisco)

- A feeling of belonging to a place, a community, and a life that does not exclude the liberty to make decisions—and sometimes move around and explore with no local obligations.
- A clean and healthy environment, vibrant with the diversity of life, and
- The perspective that our children will have similar opportunities.
- A secure means of subsistence that can cover our basic material needs and give us respect in the community.
- A supportive family, friends, and a pacific, safe community that allows us to explore and develop our capabilities for establishing loving relationships.

This author assures us that the items listed are compatible with natural and technological means in all societies, which is a relief to know, since so many years have passed since the calculations that Buckminster Fuller used to ensure us of the same thing in the decade of the 70s.

In a recent book[3] that bears the subtitle *A Better World is Possible*, the members of the International Globalization Forum (IGF) continued the reflection they began in Seattle on a "sustainable society" and reduced the fundamental issues that characterize a functional society to ten. They begin with a **"New Democracy"**—expression in which the word "new" refers to something more than the usual election of representatives. Taking into account situations like the one in which the directors of companies are guided only by immediate earnings that come from the harvesting of trees, for example, without taking into account the cost implied by flooding or alterations in the availability of water that their decision may bring to others, or more generally, considering the fact that today issues of public health, work, environment, or the rules of international commerce are the result of pressure exerted by companies through secret business done in

---

[3]*Alternatives to Economic Globalization. A Better World is Possible.* Report from the International Globalization Forum

remote cities in which the interests of those on whose shoulders rest the costs of the decisions made are not taken into account, the authors of this book see the need for a system of government "that gives those who will be affected by the consequences the right to vote in said decisions". It is more common today than ever—as pointed out—that we have institutionalized a type of property called "in-absentia" in which the stockholders, in whose names the companies act, are not responsible for the damage that the actions may bring on others - no matter how rhetorically democracy is exalted as the dominating spirit of developed countries.

In second place, the authors of *Alternatives to Economic Globalization* introduce the term subsidiarity in reference to the principle that says that it is better to have local control over decisions that pertain to a given region so that "only when the necessary action cannot be satisfied normally, should the power and the activity be transferred to the next higher level in the region, the nation, or the world. In this way the principle that states that sovereignty lies with the people and that legitimate authority flows up from the people will be respected, so that authority in levels that are the furthest from the administration is subsidiary or subordinated to local and citizen authority. In other words, this principle recognizes the inherent right to self-determination in communities and nations within the limits of non-infringement on other communities."

This point, as the previous one, is about a movement contrary to the excesses of hierarchic dominion, so present in the violation of democracy as well as in the violation of self-government in favor of excessively centralized governments.

In third place, the authors of the Forum on Globalization suggest a principle of **Sustainable Ecology**: the satisfaction of the real needs of those who live now must be procured, without compromising the capacity of future generations to satisfy their needs, without causing the richness of life to dwindle and without altering natural systems of self-renovation of the planet.

Just as we can say that the first two issues are antidotes for oppression, this third issue finds us holding the antidote for the lack of care we show for our descendants, on one hand, and for nature on the other. The formulation of this principle is inspired, naturally, in what is happening now, as globalization causes damage to the environment because of excessive consumption, excessive exploitation of resources and problems of waste elimination.

The next issue, which the authors call **Common Inheritance**, makes reference to "the resources that make up the collective right of our species and that must be shared equally among all." By common resources they refer not only to water, air, earth, forests and fish on which the lives of all depend, but also to public services that governments provide for their populations in questions of health, education, safety and prevision.

It is natural that everything that has to do with health— socially and individually, and not only psychologically, but also biologically—is something that is, in the end, understood in terms of pathologies and problems. In this case, the authors see fit to formulate the topic of "common resources" in the light of excessive privatization in our era of globalized economy. As in the case of the issues mentioned before, the underlying issued is love, and we can say that it is the healthy loving disposition of human beings that makes us aware of natural rights. "The intentions of people or companies to monopolize ownership of an essential resource that is part of our common inheritance, like water, certain varieties of seeds, or a forest, in exclusion of the needs of others should be considered unacceptable."

The next topic is **Diversity**, and the authors come to their conclusion by contemplating the impoverishment of biological diversity, on one hand, and on the other the cultural homogenization that the business world brings with it. In respect to this diversity it seems to me that only the perception of values intrinsic to nature or to culture can inspire a protest against the apparent advantages and conveniences that commerce finds in transforming things into homogenous products.  What would an alienated person know of these products?  With how much passion can an alienated person defend cultural diversity, architectural styles, languages or ideas when they have succumbed to the addiction of a competitive company?

The next principle that the authors of the Global Forum identify is **Human Rights**.  They begin by pointing out that in 1948 the governments of the world jointly adopted the United Nations Declaration of Human Rights that established certain fundamental rights such as a satisfactory level of life in matters of health and well-being, which includes food, clothing, housing, medical care and necessary social services - including unemployment insurance.   The authors observe, nevertheless, that the debate on Human Rights in the United States has been focused specifically on civil and political rights while not attending to economic, social and cultural rights.  For example: if we agree that every individual has the right to potable water, we would have to conclude that the water should not be privatized to be later resold at market prices, and that it should be the obligation of government to guarantee access to it. "We recognize that many governments are corrupt and irresponsible, but that hasn't forced us into the needed conclusion that the private sector should guarantee our rights."

The following issue is similar, since it refers also to Human Rights in matters of **Work and Jobs:**  the right to work, the right to choose a profession, to find fair and favorable working conditions, and the right to protection in cases of unemployment.

Also, the next issue, referring to non-harmful foods, is an issue that falls under Human Rights and that has been violated lately due to exploitative tendencies that have surpassed the voice of solidarity.

Then, the members of the mentioned forum speak about **Equality** as an alternative to the abyss that is always present between rich and poor countries, as well as to the distance between the poor and the rich within the majority of countries—and between men and women.  They point out that economic globalization has adversely and disproportionately affected women, since they are the ones who make up the majority of workers in global production chains, in factories or in plantations, and are also the main source of domestic workers, even though they may receive no pay for these services. They add: "And just as in the lowest level within the production chains we find mainly women, the high executives and global bureaucrats are nearly all men, reinforcing the unequal pay scales."

It is easy to agree with these authors when they say that the resulting social rupture and tension make up one of the greatest threats to peace and safety in the world.

Greater equality, among nations and within them, would strengthen democracy and the forming of sustainable communities.

Lastly, the authors formulate the principle called **"Precaution"** in reaction to the current situation that requires governments to show categorical proof of damage before being able to suspend the distribution of certain products or the application of certain technologies. Such a policy is antagonistic to the duty of governments to protect their citizens and if it had been in effect in the 50s, the FDA would not have been able to forbid the use of thalidomide, which caused deformations in thousands of babies born in countries where the drug had been approved. They say: "Adopting the principle of precaution is essential if citizens are to have the right to decide through their representatives what risks to take and what risks to subject the environment to."

It seems clear to me that all of this is simply the expression of common sense and a healthy attitude. It is not necessary to be an expert to agree with what seems to be the natural expression of intuition guided by justice, and what seems to us to be simply a question of humanity or a condition that is free from the parasitic infection of the mind by greed, deceit and other aberrations. If speaking to these things requires a certain intellectual sophistication, it is only because said sophistication is needed to penetrate the rhetoric of fraudulence that cloaks the current state of things. The conditions or principles listed by the members of the International Globalization Forum, therefore, are perfectly congruent with the description of health that I proposed earlier when I emphasized that they make up corollaries to the three great values pronounced in my "three-brained theory of love: the search for happiness, the appreciation of kindness and the capacity for reverence."

But, is it not possible to derive some political inspiration from the vision of our three-fold structure - as three-brained beings born of a mother and a father? Or, to ask this in a different way: besides formulating what is desirable by contemplating concrete undesirable realities, could we not formulate more universal corollaries through the three-part model of the mind and generally conceiving what the world would be like if it were governed by "three voices"—meaning by considering the needs and contributions of our Three?

Here are my thoughts on the alternative to our patriarchal form of government.

Since it is not even necessary to state the following, it makes a good starting point: the patriarchal government is hierarchical and is formed by chains of command. If we wish to go from the domination of an "absolute father" to a balance of powers among the three components of our nature, it means to go from the hierarchical organization to a heterarchical organization of society (just as our mind is organized).

The patriarchal form of government contrasts with the "matristic" form, which still exists today in matrilineal and tribal cultures, in which authority rests with the group or community instead of with charismatic chiefs or experts (as referred to by Engels in his concept of "original communism"). Naturally, throughout history we have seen polarization between supporters of centralized authority and supporters of popular or democratic authority, but since the history of the civilized world is patriarchal, the democratic ideal has been expressed less in our political reality than has the hierarchical ideal.

There is no doubt nevertheless, that the majority of people are in agreement that not only is tyranny by individuals bad, but that tyranny by a group would also be bad. The historian Jacques Barzun and others have lamented a growing "demotic" tendency—meaning a situation in which the weight of mediocrity or vulgarity is felt more and more in decisions that involve us. And not only is balance between the expert and the will of the governed important: there is no doubt that it is also important that the power of the individual over his own acts not be trampled—by government or by the community.

Totila Albert thought that our archaic society, previous to the matristic period, could have been in essence a "filiarchy" in which not only did the will of the young prevail over the old, but individual strength and self-affirmation prevailed over tradition and tribal life. The dream of anarchists like Kropotkin and Bakunin would also be filiarchies. They trusted that the authority of individuals over their own lives would result in social balance and not in the chaos imagined by supporters of authoritarian and repressive control.

It could well be said that in a society of awakened beings, collective organismic regulation would allow self-government in each individual and thereby a magnificent concert—but to speak of beings that are awake, healthy or complete is to speak of three-brained beings. Only in a world like that could the will of each individual be congruent with the dictates of love and wisdom which would then cause us to form networks of solidarity and functional authority through which anarchy would respond spontaneously in the form of heterarchy: heterarchy between anarchy, hierarchy and democracy.

But then, in speaking of democracy we must remember that the only relatively participative democracy that we have seen in the civilized world was in Athens—possible only because the people who deliberated then in the agora were few enough that they all knew each other.

Naturally, nations require, because of their size, a representative democracy. But what would democracy be able to do if the candidates were subject to political commitments and not economic pressure?

It seems to me that due to the need to efficiently channelize the voice of the community, sovereign nations become an obstacle, and the only virtue of the current transnational empire could perhaps be the fact that it frees us from the power and vices of local government. Now all that is needed is for the "co-emperors" to decide to use their power in sincere service to the common good.

Our current political state could be described as the weakening of the political machines of nations which is causes problems because there is no balance between the world of business and traditional political authority. It is to be expected that this sad situation give way to another in which the voice of the masses can find a new way to be heard—giving way to a true participative democracy. To a certain point we can say that this development is sketched in the proliferation of non-governmental organizations, through which citizens are trying to attend to social, ecological, and other needs that governments ignore, but the limited economic power that these institutions have correspondingly limits their effectiveness. Perhaps it is conceivable that someday small units of self-government will emerge—comparable to the ancient city-states—from whose coordination and federation into larger geographical units (today much easier because of progress in cybernetics and communication) will come a new form of expression of popular will that would be required as a counterpart or harmonic complement to good leadership and freedom for citizens.

For those who find themselves faced with the responsibility of piloting our "spaceship Earth" in the future and who are interested in looking at a map, as well as for those who work to draw these maps, I wish to contribute this very simple idea: that our transition should be, in essence, from an undercover tyranny that hides behind the rhetoric of democracy to a government in which the wise men, the voice of the community and the capacity for self-government operate in balance—as respect for individuality requires. In order to better understand this thought, I would like to quote a historical mention of the same topic in a passage from my yet unpublished book *The Problem of Civilization:*

"If the patriarchal society depends on a hierarchy presided by the institution of the State—that is, the control over individuals and groups by a few who have more expertise and, in the best of cases, are better equipped—while matristic cultures have been characterized by the control that the community or clan has on the individual, we can imagine that in the times of archaic nomadic and filial-centered collectors, an individual's control over himself was dominant and there was relative independence from group ties and exclusion from any political regime of authority.

Can we not, then, conceive the alternative to the patriarchal regime as one in which there is a heterarchic relationship between these aspects of political life—on the intra-psychic, family and socio-cultural levels?

We well know the exaggerated problem of centralized authority through our long history of dictatorships, and we can imagine the problems of a group dictatorship—as in the Marxist proposal of a proletarian dictatorship like in matristic cultures—that our ancestors preferred to leave in the past. At the same time, we are also familiar with the negative connotations of the word "anarchy" that has come to mean something similar to chaos. But we are just as familiar with the positive aspects of the three forms of government. The authoritarian proposal that is revealed to us precisely in the word *"hierarchy"*—which makes an allusion to sacredness, whereas the democratic proposal of "a government by the people and for the people" has become our contemporary ideal, while the libertarian and anarchic proposal of anarchic self-government was—we should mention—the vision that the prophets had in the form of the "kingdom of God," where no authority would be placed in competition with divine will, which individuals would be able to recognize in their hearts.

As is characteristic of the structural hierarchy in the central nervous system, where higher centers control lower centers, the intellect normally guides action and the prefrontal cortex controls even the intellect. It would seem that a healthy social regime should not be so frantically democratic and go to the extreme of eliminating all principles of authority; and it seems to me equally as obvious that even the balance between the central government (be it in groups, schools or regions) and the democratic government of the community would be an aberration if the individual were trampled by this combination of solicitations from "above" and from the environment. It is necessary then to stave off this type of aberration through a theoretical model that contemplates healthy individualism; meaning one that includes a certain dose of individual authority over the individual's own life.

Once such a vision of a healthy society protects us not only from military dictatorships but also from public opinion or market laws, it is clear that freedom will be made up by two different dimensions: the freeing of the "inner child" that operates in each of us through our capacity for organismic regulation (which goes from the wisdom of the body to the instincts and intuition that allow us to follow our most subtle inner voices) and the freeing of the "popular will" that in turn expresses our healthy feeling of brotherhood and solidarity.

And with this I end my ramblings on the Albertinian vision of a "balance of three" and all that is left is for me to propose that, in this balance, what we call our spiritual or divine nature resides and expresses itself. Or, to say it in another way, each of our inner persons is divine, but their sacred character is hidden to us when the regime of inner tyranny of society and the patriarchal mind denigrates the animal or instinctive aspect in us, enslaves the maternal loving aspect and turns the cognitive aspect of our minds into a monstrously insensitive thinking machine.

Today we know that the integrative faculty that can exert inhibiting control on each of our brains is something like a fourth brain, found in a precise region of the cerebral cortex: the prefrontal area—that extends from the mythical region of the third eye, found in religious iconography, to the base and interior of the brain, all the way to the limbic brain. In phenomenological terms, we could say that "the voice" in our inner lives that can bring harmony to the relationship between father, mother and child is not really a voice, but a silence. This is what I wanted to allude to when I announced these pages by referring to a "pyramidal model" of the conscience. If we imagine a pyramid with a triangular base, we can say that the three angles of the base, sitting on the ground, correspond to something that is identifiable—specifically our brains or inner persons. The vortex, by contrast, rising above concrete existence, is pure transcendence or (to say it in a different way) pure nothingness. It is the capacity to become nothing through which we become whole; nothingness allows us enough un-identification in respect to each of our centers— thinking, will and feeling—so that one of them does not become a type of dictator that rises above the others, breaking the unity of our psyche. And only by learning to empty our minds—or un-identifying ourselves from its contents through the practice of detachment implied in meditation, can we transcend compulsive thought, calm our passions and at the same time free ourselves from the obsessive search for pleasure and the obsessive avoidance of pain that characterizes the ordinary mind.

## 3.    What Can We Do?

*"Nevertheless, in the midst of this lack of harmony without precedent, we are faced with an opportunity that we may not have again for another millennium: the opportunity to create a society that reflects our deepest values. In a world that seems to be heading in a million directions at once, we can and must choose a direction, a focus, an intention. In no other time in history has it been so clear that the future depends on us."*

*"The Creation of a World that Works for Everyone"*
Vaclav Havel

### *Sins of Society*

There are people who have dealt with huge problems that, in spite of their enormous importance and multiform symptoms, are only symptoms, in turn, of a deeper malady, facets of the more fundamental collective problem that in previous chapters I interpreted as the result of an imbalance between our brains or inner persons.  So, emotionally moved by the tradition of love through violence, by the repression of wise spontaneity of life, by the commercialization of the world and government by money, etc., some have given themselves over to causes such as non-violence, pacifism, the fight for freedom over oppression, the mission of sounding the alarm on the technocratic plutocracy in the commercial military system, the fight against exploitation, the campaign against corruption and other crusades.

Before examining the practical consequences that come with the idea that the fundamental cause of our condition is found in the patriarchal structure of our minds and society, I will talk about some of these huge problems that are found on a more evident plain.

I have spoken previously about the nine aspects of our social pathology in *The Enneagram of Society*, where I proposed that each of these problems corresponds to one of

the deficient motivations or "capital sins"[1] in the individual
mind, and therefore it is also reasonable to consider them
capital sins or evils of society[2]. Now, however, I will limit
myself to the consideration of five of these collective
problems—since these five are the ones that most define the
structure of our institutions:  authoritarianism, institutional
inertia, mercantilism, exploitation, and repression.

Although in each case I will share my opinion on how
we can overcome these evils, I hope to also communicate my
pessimism as to how much we can improve our condition
using known resources.  I suspect that even a new Hercules
would be unable to cut off the nine heads of our collective
patriarchal ego, and I think it is time that we aim for the heart
of the beast.  What this implies I will talk about in the third
and last part of this chapter.

## *Violence*

Intimately related to masculine dominance, violence has
accompanied the patriarchal regime since its origins.
Certainly wars have been a characteristic trait of our history (it
has been calculated that there has been one year of peace for
each seventeen years of war) and in schools in all countries
military victories are proudly flaunted for the edification of
generations of children.  It would seem that there are few
things that have been given as much importance in history text
books as these military conquests and acts of subjugation.
Nevertheless, we know that war, along with slavery,
originated in the Bronze Age some 6000 years ago and is,
therefore, not intrinsic to human nature.  Patriarchal war is,
intrinsic to sovereign states and is brought to life in armies.
But these are only the organs of an implicit philosophy of
power that is part of our way of life.  Today, violence

---

[1]The ones from the Gregorian system that survived in Catechism plus
two others, in accordance with Christian esoterism of the "Fourth
Way."
[2]This implies the interpretation of other severe problems, such as
poverty and injustice, as derivatives.

increases as a response to the violence that is implicit in the injustice of a system that we have not chosen. And if what I say is not obvious, it should be enough just to contemplate the history of the aggressive colonialism of our civilized world as written about in the works of critics like Chomsky. And this colonialism continues today, wearing a mask of perfectionism.

The war budget is an important component of our economic, medical, educational and other problems, even though this expense is convenient for certain industrialists and it can be said that the human cost of war implies violence that is none the lesser than the destruction of lives on the battle front. Imperialism has always been an agent of exploitation and in spite of its rhetoric it has not let up since its origins in ancient times. On the contrary: it could well be said that modern capitalist imperialism—with its globalization rhetoric, its puppet governments, and its occasional support for state terrorism[3]—is the most destructive factor we have seen in history to date. The consideration of international relation policies of apparently advanced and exemplary countries should be enough to make us see how much greater violence is than solidarity and how far we really are from having reached the condition of being a healthy society.

But this term is also used to indicate a contemporary State model that is obliged to go beyond ideology and policies of "legal" repression (consented to by the traditional legal framework) and use "non-conventional methods," extensive and intensive, to annihilate political opposition, whether armed or unarmed.

---

[3]Bonasso says in his prologue to Chomsky's book on this subject that "the phenomenon of State terrorism is as old as the society of classes itself," but that this expression, which at the same time names and qualifies the phenomenon, is relatively new. In his words:
We speak of "State terrorism" to differentiate it from just "terrorism" that involves groups or individuals that do not precisely have the repressive power of the State and use indiscriminate violence to express their opposition to this power and the efforts to establish it.

State terrorism is always shameful because it is always trapped in the same contradiction; it has to disseminate its cruelest and most aberrant practices in order to generalize terror and ensure domination, but it must, at the same time, deny being the author of the same in order not to transgress internal and international legal norms that ensure—in theory— the respect for human rights.

Whether it is the armed forces or traditional civil institutions, the "dirty war" that is being fought against the opposition no longer obeys the capricious whim of the traditional dictator so often described in Latin American literature. Power has transitory individual representations that are subordinated to abstract and anonymous bodies. The objectives and strategy are no longer derived from the intuition or decision of old time caudillos, like the Francos or the Trujillos. Even more so, terrorist power models are designed in "war schools"...The comparison between crisis and counterinsurgency is not latent, precisely because this "higher phase" of counterinsurgency that is State terrorism comes from the need of imperialism and their allies to contain—by new methods—the popular masses that resist continued payment of the higher cost of the economic crisis, which reduces geographical space for State terrorism to the least favored countries on Earth, in other words, the Third World. This means: State terrorism is a type of merchandise destined for the condemned of the Earth.

Violence is not only expressed, not even mainly expressed, in assassinations and wars. The essence of violence is found in insensitivity in the face of pain and death of others, a soulless condition that also becomes manifest in decisions that put gain before life. The enormous amount of injustice makes up the expression of implicit violence, that, perceived as such, generates, in turn, violence—from elementary school to terrorism. And, above all, gives way to a game of implicit violence—of masquerading humanity— inherent in the decision of the world to rule itself in accordance with the interests of rich businessmen at the expense of great suffering, poverty, destruction and helplessness on the part of an alarmingly growing fraction of the population.

In his book *Dirty Truths*, which is about those things that happen around us but that we are forbidden to mention because mentioning them would be risky for the reputation of the person who does so, Michael Parenti proposes that in the richest country of our current world there are catastrophic events that reflect both the poor functioning of society and tragic carelessness of the common good on the part of decision makers. He cites, for example, that each year 27 thousand North Americans commit suicide, 13 million are victims of crimes, 37 million regularly use medication to control their emotional state, 80 million have sought out psychological help, one million children run away from home as a result of abuse, 5 million are in jail or on parole, 4.5 million suffer from malnutrition and between 7 and 12 million are out of work. He concludes that: "if we consider only those that have suffered physical or sexual abuse, a serious incapacity or a serious deprivation such as malnutrition and lack of housing, and only those that die from suicide, homicide, physical aggression, drug abuse, alcohol abuse, industrial or traffic accidents or sexually transmitted disease, we still have a number of over 19 million victims. Later he summarizes: "in the twelve years during which 58,000 Americans died in Vietnam, a few million died prematurely in the United States of non-natural and often violent causes." He also mentions that "a government study has concluded that the air we breathe, the water we drink and the food we eat are today the main causes of death in the United States"; he goes on to say that "none of the ciphers include the unhappiness, abandonment, and long-term emotional wounds that millions of loved ones, friends and family members of victims suffer," and because of all this he concludes that "contrary to what official declarations say, *we are facing a hidden holocaust, a social pathology of gigantic dimensions and consequences.*"

On an individual scale, the corrective for violence is, of course, the Christian formula of responding to aggression with love: "Turning the other cheek." But this is not something that has been practiced yet in the politics of our "western Christian civilization"—even though Lincoln insisted that the best way to destroy an enemy is to make him your friend, and even though Tolstoy inspired Ghandi. (It is well known that his conviction that the old law "an eye for an eye" would only result in generalized blindness in the world was able to inspire the most notable pacific revolution in history.)

In view of the brutal situation of our contemporary history in which powerful countries trample those who resist economic submission, pacifism could seem to be senseless and inoperative, but it is also clear that we should aspire to a less violent future and be creatively interested in how to reach it. This is congruent with the objective that we put a limit on implicit violence in our economic system and the lack of sensitivity by which we are destroying the environment. Nevertheless, the greatest problem that we face in wanting to change our destructive habits, is the generalized immaturity of people with respect to the development of love. I thing that the birth of psychotherapy in the past century could be the announcement of a difference, particularly as self-help groups multiply and become more effective, but psychotherapy and spiritual traditions fall short—since transformation is difficult and demands intense motivation and sacrifices. Our best alternative, it seems, is to prevent instead of cure, through public health and especially through education.

### Repression, Moralism, Police Mentality, and Xenophobia

Just as I've spoken of violence and exploitation together, since these characteristics happen together in the psychology of the individual, I will now talk about the topic of repression and the topic of moralism or criminalizing mentality, the hypertrophy of the police mentality that is associated with it, and nationalism understood as an arbitrary group "superiority complex." Also, in this case individual psychology shows us how intimately these traits are related.

Although the word repression in psychological language still holds the meaning Freud gave it of avoiding conscious access to certain mental contents, it is good to remember that the social meaning of the term refers more to action than to consciousness:  it is a mechanism by which authority controls the conduct of individuals by dictating what they should do and punishing disobedience.  But the word "repression" is not enough to evoke the characteristic form in which this mechanism functions in society, which is the *criminalization* of transgression and glorification of the proposals that authorities make through what I am here calling *moralism*.

In order to be able to make demands, people who are characteristically demanding invoke certain ideals and at the same time devalue those who don't comply. Socially this situation manifests itself as a situation similar to the crusades, where in virtue of supposed spiritual or cultural superiority the "infidels" were trampled.  But we don't have to use such distant historical examples, since the phenomenon in question appears each time nationalist tendencies are expressed. It is an error to look at nationalism as an expression of love for one's own people. No matter how much that rhetoric is used to justify it, nationalism is the collective equivalent to egotism on an individual scale, with its usual rationalizations.

Once more, it is all about a tendency intimately associated to masculine dominance and when, from the perspective of the centuries, we consider the case of the conquistadors that felt authorized to enslave or destroy the South American Indians in view of their supposed barbarianism or the nobility of their own very Christian emperor, it becomes transparent how the exaltation of their own values became a pretext or rationalization for greed and the tendency toward exploitation.  But we have very limited consciousness of the measure in which moralism in our own days—meaning the exaltation of our own values—is serving us as an instrument of repression and power.

That psychology has been able to shed light on this individually allows us to better understand what happens in society. What psychology has shown us about the people in whom the moralizing attitude is a main characteristic is specifically clarifying:  those who in academic language are diagnosed with "obsessive personalities" and who in the psychology of the Ennea-types are called perfectionists.  It was Freud who for the first time described the personality that is exaggeratedly clean, honest and orderly, and who observed how the exaggerated pulchritude that he designated at the time as the "anal character" was developed in answer to a premature demand for sphincter control.  The child has introjected the exaggerated aversion toward his own excrement, and has compensated his experience of being dirty by a chronic attempt at reparation.

Naturally, when speaking of moralism I am talking about something that is different from morality, reserving the term for a type of Puritanism or pharisaism that is intrinsically repressive and exploiting.  Sub-commander Marcos admirably described this use of morals in the function of exploitation in a passage the he attributes to collaboration between his daemon and Berthold Brecht.  I cite:

"If sharks were men"—the boss's youngest daughter asked Mr. K., "Would they behave better with the smaller fish?"

"Of course"—Mr. K. responded—"If sharks were men they would build huge boxes in the sea for the little fish, with all kinds of food inside, both from plant and animal materials. They would be concerned that the boxes always had fresh water and they would adopt all kinds of sanitary measures. If, for example, a fish hurt a fin, it would be bandaged immediately so that the fish would not die on the sharks too early.  So that the small fish wouldn't be sad, there would be, once in a while, huge aquatic parties, because after all, the fish would taste better if they were happy.  There would also be schools in the boxes.  These schools would teach the fish to swim into the sharks' jaws.  They would need to know about geography to be able to locate the large sharks that are lying about.  The main thing, naturally, would be the moral formation of the little fish.  They would be taught that there is nothing more important or beautiful for a small fish than to sacrifice itself happily; and they would also be taught to have faith in the sharks, and to believe them when they say that they are building a better future for them. They would be told that the future that awaited them would be guaranteed if they learned to obey. The little fish would learn to stay away from low passions, as well as from any materialistic, egotistical or Marxist inclination. If any little fish were to show any of those tendencies, the other fish would have to report them immediately to the sharks. If the sharks were men, they would naturally have wars with other sharks to conquer boxes and other sharks' little fish. Besides, each shark would oblige its own little fish to fight those wars. Each shark would teach its little fish that between them and the little fish that belong to other sharks there are huge differences. Even though all the little fish are mute, it would be proclaimed that if they are still, they are all still in very different languages and that is why they would never understand each other. For each little fish that dies in a war a couple of enemy little fish, the ones who are still in another language, would receive a medal and would be called heroes. If sharks were men, they would also have art. There would be beautiful paintings of shark teeth in wonderful colors, and jaws that look like gardens in which it would be wonderful to play. Theaters on the bottom of the sea would depict heroic little fish enthusiastically going into the sharks' jaws and the music would be so beautiful that, in its honor and lulled by the most delicious thoughts, like in a dream, the little fish would flock, led by a band, to the jaws. This would be their religion, if sharks were men.

This religion would teach that true life begins for the little fish in the sharks' stomachs. Also, if sharks were men, the little fish would no longer be all the same, as they are now.

Some would occupy offices, which would put them above others. The little fish that were a bit larger would even be allowed to swallow the smaller ones. Sharks would watch this practice with attention, because that way they would have larger fish to eat. The fattest fish, which would be the only ones to occupy certain positions, would be in charge of keeping order among the other little fish, and they would be teachers or officers, engineers specialized in building boxes, etc. In a word: if sharks were men there would finally be culture in the sea."

All civilizations have been repressive, and if ours seems to be the exception it is because we have perfected the repressive operation to such a degree that is no longer obvious, and a type of unconsciousness allows us to feel better. But jails are becoming a problem, since they are fuller and multiplying. Naturally this takes away from productivity in society and costs a lot in maintenance, and we all know how jails contribute to the deterioration of prisoners and their families, especially now when mental health issues and the evolution of consciousness have become so critical.

I mention jails not only because of the fact that, over time, legislation becoming more and more condemning is a great tragedy, making it easier for minor crimes, like the possession of small quantities of marijuana, to result in the loss of lives or mental deterioration in solitary cells because of "lack of cooperation" or complications in the lives of inmates or because jails are recently being privatized, becoming just another business. I mention them also because they make up a symptom that shows us the paradoxical truth of the police mentality in the campaign against crime that ends up contributing to criminality. As has been said, "the moral majority is neither of the two (neither moral nor the majority), and people have realized how in the past the war against the supposed red threat and the more recent war on drugs reflect a desperate attempt on the part of a dysfunctional system to defend itself. Even schools are starting to seem like prisons, since children, perhaps less alienated from their instinctiveness and their intuition, react with violence against the authoritarian character of what is offered to them as education.

In effect, children perceive more and more the irrelevance of an instruction that has little to do with their existential situation and they rebel against teachers that don't seem to be awakened enough to life to realize this irrelevance—which results in them sometimes, in their impotence, behaving destructively. This then confirms to the authorities that they are correct in thinking that the children are the problem and in trying to force order through the use of growing power.

On an individual level, the repression of instinct and control of conduct of others is made possible through the building of what would seem to be noble ideals that individuals are proud to hold and preach. In a similar way, repression is justified on a social level through a feeling of moral superiority and a conviction of being right, which justifies indignation. When this superiority becomes condemning toward others in the same group, it leads to criminalization. When it is used against other groups, we call it prejudice, xenophobia or nationalism.

If the repressive character of society is a problem, if moralism and high-sounding patriotism are archaic mechanisms to hide our injustice and if the apparently well-intentioned police tendency of our modern world is only rationalized violence at the service of a questionable authority and in defense of the status quo (when what we most need is evolution), what can we do?

What can we do in the face of an empire founded on prejudice that sees barbarianism or criminality where it sees fit to in order to protect its own superiority as a class or a nation? Naturally a lot has been tried and in these attempts slavery has been officially abolished and, in more civilized countries, blacks and whites can ride in the same elevators; but the fight for civil liberties is problematic, and the questioning of nationalism is way beyond just problematic. Neither can go far without progress made in the area of consciousness. And although art throughout generations has helped people to be more conscious of what is happening around them, consciousness in the end run is an individual issue.

On an individual level practically the only cure for moralism is found in deep-reaching psychotherapy, since moralism (whether unconscious manipulation or hypocrisy) cannot survive in the presence of self-knowledge. Nietzsche,

from whom Freud inherited his understanding of the defensive
and compulsive nature of conventional morals, saw an answer
to this excess in the Dionysian spirit[4], and I think that nothing
could be more exact. I think also that the Dionysian spirit has
begun to penetrate the world through psychotherapy—
particularly since the birth of humanistic psychotherapy. But,
as in the case of violence, we cannot expect psychotherapy to
help more than a minority. It would be necessary to take the
competencies of this work into the world of education. I also
think that with respect to the liberation of spontaneity and the
increase in authenticity in people of the world, there is no
greater hope than a freer and freeing education that is geared
toward the forming of those "three-brained harmonic beings"
that Gurdjieff[5] conceived.

## *Authoritarianism*

Authority has been a center column of civilization since the
beginning through the establishment of hierarchies of power
during the time of the first large cities. Since then, the many
being subject to the few has been a characteristic of the
civilized world—even though today faith in the more
authentically monarchic regimes has all but disappeared. The
democratic ideal is professed and monarchy is considered an
abomination.

It could be argued that control of the masses by the
few is no less common in modern nations than in ancient
monarchic regimes, except that it is enforced in a less visible

---

[4]Author's note: It is thought that the Dionysian religion—or cult of
Dionysus, a god who was persecuted and who went mad, died and was
reborn—came before the religion of the Olympian gods. It is
characterized by the spirit of surrendering to spontaneity and respect
for pleasure as well as faith in the natural order. Nietzsche contrasted
the Dionysian spirit, symbolized by wine and drunkenness, with the
Apollonian spirit, characterized by lucidity and control.
[5]Founder of the Institute for the Harmonic Development of Man whose
ideas became known mainly through the Russian scientist and writer,
Ouspensky.

way—combining an apparently democratic form of government (in which citizens can, each so many years, express their preference for one or another candidate, generally a wealthy person) with sophisticated manipulation of public opinion. In what measure, though, can we say that modern democracies represent governments "by the people and for the people"? Surely it would be more correct to describe them as cases like the ones Spanish poet and journalist, Federico Jimenez Losantos, has called silent dictatorships in the title of one of his books that is precisely about totalitarian mechanisms in European democracy.

Before continuing with these considerations about authoritarianism, of which exploiting violence and criminalizing repression are the weapons of choice, I want to open a parenthesis to introduce some notions about the psychology of the Ennea-types.

Throughout this presentation I have had the figure of the Enneagram present, even though all the readers are not familiar with it, so now I think it would be useful to make it explicit: a geometric figure that an esoteric school, probably Mesopotamian, proposes as allusive to certain regularities in the laws of nature and that is then viable as an applicable map for diverse things and processes. It consists of nine points along a circumference that are connected as seen in the illustration following.

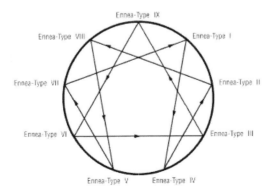

Intimately related to the tree of life of the Kabbalah, the Enneagram was brought to the western world by Gurdjieff; but it was a Bolivian, Oscar Ichazo, who later presented to the Chilean Association of Psychologists the essence of the psychological applications of this method that he called Protoanalysis.

When using the Enneagram as a map of the basic passions (or as would be said today, of the motivations based on deficiency, or emotions based on losses) lust or thirst for intensity (dominant in violent people) is found in point 8, and anger (a characteristic that is not always evident in perfectionists, whose moral defect is disguising morality) is represented in point 1. When entering the province of authoritarianism, we are talking about the personality in which the dominant characteristic is fear, at point 6, which is situated on the left-hand vortex of the central triangle of the Enneagram, and I've chosen this moment to introduce these considerations with respect to the structural relationships between pathologies because in the psychology of the personality the processes that are alluded to in the central triangle (that I will talk about now) are considered more fundamental than the rest.

It is easy to understand through the abundant historical information we have today how the collective authoritarian regime came about as a result of the absolute authority of "pater familias," and how in antiquity it extended to larger groups, giving way to the first monarchies and then to empires. No wonder Totila Albert, pioneer in denouncing the patriarchal regime, wrote during the Second World War: "We have been looking for the cause of lack of union between human beings and the unsolvable lack of order that reigns over human life, and in this search the State and the Church, of course, have been criticized, but the definitive step has never been taken:  to make the creator of these institutions responsible since he is the one that arbitrarily assigned himself the right to dispose of life and death in the family, declaring himself owner and taking power over all goods."

When making "the person responsible for our institutions" an individual—naturally the male of our species —he was often called "the absolute father," an expression we can consider a personification of masculine domination, and it seems to me that to speak of "father" rather than "man" has the advantage of allowing us to allude to the family trinity (from which authority has come in society) and not only to the dominion of man over woman, but the ownership of the life of children, which has characterized classic patriarchy.

Male domination can be seen in the root of dominion of reason over emotion in most of the civilized world, as well as the dominion of exploitation over cultivation, aggression over tenderness, and competition over collaboration. But authoritarianism not only rests on reason (which justifies the exercise of its will) and on force, that associated with insensibility becomes violence: authoritarianism also uses ideality, which constitutes its natural legitimacy, and thought (ideological) control.

Much of what has been said about authoritarianism in psychology shows the imprinting of the monumental study published half-way through the last century, *The Authoritarian Personality,* in which the authors (Adorno, Sanford and Frenkel-Brunswick) describe a type of person characterized, in psychological terms, by a rigid superego, a weak ego and an alienated id (in other words, a person who is excessively oriented toward group norms and who feels that his spontaneous impulses are separate from himself, something that "happens to him."

The investigators mentioned observed that what they designated as the "authoritarian personality" and identified, using their famous "F scale" (in reference to fascism), that it was not really one, but a combination of three diverse human types. Later investigation, based on the then novel statistical technique of factorial analysis, confirmed it. In one of the forms described, the authoritarian personality was first of all like the obsessive and perfectionist personality (E1) in relation to moralism; secondly a cynical and Machiavellian type that is much like the violent and rebellious E8; while in third place like the paranoid and insecure E6 in the psychology of the Enneatypes—a character in which fear dominates.

Different from the first two characters described—the moralist and the antisocial—which are dominant characters, the most identifiable characteristic in this last fearful character is obedience to authority, and even when this character becomes dominant (as a paranoid defense against imaginary attacks) he is yet someone with a strong hierarchic sentiment, that makes him receptive to authorities, to the voice of established power or to precepts of a determined ideology.

If we transfer this psychological information to society, we can say that if violence eliminates undesirables and the police organ of society obliges citizens to behave in accordance to the dictates of a corrupt or manipulated authority, we can call "authoritarianism in itself" the faith that sustains this operation—an excessive tendency to delegate one's own power and decisions to others, particularly when these others express themselves with clear simplicity and vehemence, evoking strength and certainty.

We know that the fear of authority that is underlying in this type of submission has roots that are deeply embedded in the childhood fear of punishment that originated the inhibition of spontaneity as a reaction to the weight of blame and the need to abide by the dictates of authorities, a code that defines what is ideal and what is condemnable, in order to guarantee approval.

It could be said that when we were children it was functional for us to bide by the authority of our parents: it is part of being healthy and of our genetic and neurological programming to imitate them, feeling that they are superior, quasi-divine. This natural authority is complicated, however, when an aggressive father uses exaggerated control and intimidation. The result is no longer healthy obedience, but compulsive obedience for the person subjugated. Unfortunately, in the majority of cases, the disposition of those who we consider good boys or girls is this type of disposition, unconsciously of course, since the authoritarianism that is transmitted from parents to children is reinforced by schools. Therefore, in the light of dynamic psychology, the condition that we call normal is being submissive to authorities and not rebellious (authoritarianism backwards, we could say), a condition in which freedom is associated with anxiety and guilt.

Nothing is closer to the childhood experience of spontaneously imitating his parents than the experience of the adult who enthusiastically follows a charismatic authority. The word "charismatic" comes from "charisma" which in theological language refers originally to grace, but in later sociological language came to refer to a person with characteristics that are more than human, extraordinary.

It seems to me that excessive secularization of the notion of charismatic authority has led to the fact that the expression in general evokes the phenomenon of excessive authority that comes from immaturity and the excessive need for a father on the part of people who have tendencies to idealize and see exceptional attributes in ordinary people and even in opportunistic charlatans. This is exactly what happens in insecure or fanatical personalities when they are moved by excessive fear, people who are abundant in our authoritarian culture. It would be convenient, however, for this not to cause us to forget that even in adult life there are functional authority issues (or, as Fromm called them, rational authority issues) in which a person recognizes the pertinence of following the advice or lead of a person who seems wiser or simply better informed. The relationship between friends (as Aristotle observed) is precisely one in which one person feels attracted by the greater maturity and virtue of the other and emulates him through implicit learning. The phenomenon is more obvious in situations where a spiritual guide or a great leader is followed. I don't think we should consider the ancient kings—the priests of Babylon or the Pharaohs of ancient Egypt—as simple manipulators of the idealizing disposition of the masses. It seems more that their strong level of authority would suggest the recognition of something      genuinely extraordinary in them: a high level of personal development that in a certain sense made them "superhuman," and it is natural that people intuitively recognize the greater capacity to judge or decide in issues of the common good on the part of a person who has reached superior consciousness.

Max Weber observed a transition from charismatic authority to "bureaucratic authority" in the history of religious movements, and I think that this type of transition can be seen in the evolution of authority in the world throughout the history of civilization in general.

At the beginning, spiritual authority coincided with temporal authority. Later the monarchic institution separated itself from the priesthood and the priests controlled the kings. Later, the kings achieved greater power—although it was less charismatic and more violent. Dante, toward the end of his life, at a moment when the power of the Pope was superior to that of the kings, wrote *De Monarchia* which holds that the balance between the empire and the papal state guaranteed the health of the respective authority, but the corruption of the spiritual authority was already as obvious as the brutality of the emperors. The greater freedom of opinion and access to information that our times allow us make us unable to contemplate history without seeing how problematic governing and church institutions have been and how they continue to promote bureaucratizing and corrupting processes.

Since the Renaissance, it is true that there has been a progressive liberation, but it is curious to note that we haven't left behind bad government or been able to say that we are any closer to a just world, in spite of the notable evolution of society toward a democratic vision and the transition from traditional monarchies toward republican regimes.

It is impossible to deny that the 60s represented a huge leap forward in the history of authoritarianism, but even though the anti-authoritarian sentiment persists in our crypto-fascist times, its main manifestation may be the disinterest of citizens in political issues. This is expressed in the title of a book written by a North American journalist Jim Hightower: *If the Gods Wanted Us to Vote, They Would Give Us*

*Candidates.* No matter how true it may be that respect for the authority of the father figure has been lost, that the patriotic heroes have been considerably unidealized, and ideologies provoke mistrust, it would be a mistake to think that the patriarchy has died. It has only gone into a type of agony because the unidealization of authority delegitimizes it. Centralized control is as strong as ever, even though it has been gradually and surreptitiously displaced from politicians to the world of business—particularly to a few giant companies that control a large proportion of the riches in the world.

This new authority is so lacking in charisma that our intuition dubs it as illegitimate and it is allowed to function only in a hidden, anonymous and masked fashion—through political institutions and the force of the law, as well as through the "laws of supply and demand." But it is not true that the market is free or that the liberal dream of Adam Smith, who conceived that the self-regulating function of the market would guarantee democracy, is coming to pass. The market today would not survive without large government contributions in the form of subsidies that have been appropriately described as "charity for the rich."

Authoritarianism survives in the contemporary world through the patriotic faith that the majorities have in the established order and in institutions (and companies and professional associations are authoritarian) even when we may think that in our times of patriarchal agony the distance between authoritarianism in itself—which implies the will to surrender to leadership—and the measure of power that our lives are subject to has grown. Not only are we disappointed in our leaders—feeling that their ideal talents are of little importance—but we are also disappointed in the ideals themselves.

The times in which the church could forbid Galileo from seeing with his own eyes is behind us because hidden oppressors do not need to mandate our thoughts: it is easier for them to influence us through fictitious reality and through the filtration of influences that is possible using bombarding through mass media[6]. And while infidels are no longer condemned to be burned at the stake or traitors decapitated, rebels and "mal-adapted people" are incarcerated at the slightest provocation. The church now prohibits freedom of thought and controls the lives of everyone just as during Nazi terrorism or Stalinism the obligation to agree with ideologies was associated with threats and terrible punishment, it seems that we have come to know the political strategy of control through ideology so well that we now suspect any important theoretical proposition (even the social sciences have come to be more interested in the accumulation of information about issues with limited scope). This "post-modern" attitude is echoed in the apparent decrease in paternal authoritarianism in families and the generalized cynicism with respect to authority in our institutions. Nevertheless, there is a strong trans-national or global imperialistic element in our world that hides behind rhetoric and some forms of democracy. It seems to me that in both the social situation and the individual psychological situation the building of an attractive but false reality has become a more effective form of repression.

Much has been said about an alternative to authoritarianism but just as a traveler that is crossing a desert can go off course following a mirage; we can lose our way by listening to the eloquent rhetoric that suggests that we have reached and established a democratic world. I remember in the 50s, when I had the opportunity to travel through Romania and Poland, how Stalinists deplored totalitarianism without suspecting that they were part of a regime that was no less totalitarian than Germany or fascist Italy. Are we not now using the word democracy in a similar way? Can we speak of a government for the people and by the people just because we vote every four or five years for one well-intentioned puppet or another? I don't think we can aspire to a true democracy without an adequate educational system, in which

---

[6] I have heard the quote from Goebbels cited: "It is not difficult to get people to say that something round is square."

communitarian sentiment is cultivated and people are helped to be free and autonomous: an education that would lead us to a healthy relationship with the interpersonal environment and feeling of belonging to a community.

As to what might be the best attitude in the presence of those who currently hold the power in the system, I wish to share a piece of advice that my old uncle, Bruno Leuschner, once told me in Santiago, in the times of the dictator, Pinochet. I always knew my uncle as an agnostic and this is the only time I ever heard him say something religious: "Don't you think, Claudio, that we should ask God to enlighten our governors? Because else wise we may want to boil them in oil."

### *Conformity and the Status Quo*

If, in individual psychology, the fearsome aspect is related to an excessive tendency to bend to the dictates of the authority, the aspect of "laziness" in which there is a disconnection from the most intimate of desires is not a completely independent issue, but a complementary one—and the relation between these aspects is represented in the Enneagram by the line that joins points 6 and 9.

In a similar way we can say that authoritarianism and conformity are complementary in the social aspect: authoritarianism could be said to contain paternal authority within society just as conformity contains the position of the obedient child, and there is no authority without subjects willing to surrender part of their own power.

Just as moralism is different from morals (making up something akin to a compulsive pseudo-morality that serves violence, a rationalization through which people or social entities ensure their desires). Conformity differs substantially from the attitude of a healthy child who responds to the wishes and advice of his parents and who builds his personality in accordance with the positive characteristics that he admires in them.

Point 9 on the Enneagram of the personality corresponds to what the Fathers of the Desert (solitary monks who derived the doctrine of capital sins) called ascidia:  a psycho-spiritual inertia that is very different from what the word "laziness" (used in the current list of capital sins) suggests.  On the social level it is easy to see how a similar psycho-spiritual inertia is manifest in the fossilization of institutions and resistance to change.

The power of the status quo increases with the size and age of the groups and we all know something about what sociologists call "the bureaucratic phenomenon"—its characteristic resistance to creative initiatives.  Another expression of the status quo is the exaggeration of conservative tendencies that, through attachment to ideas and obsolete ways of life, are in conflict with the need for continuous social evolution in an ever-changing world.

In principle, a conservative spirit and a radical spirit are both valid, since we need a healthy appreciation for wise traditions from the past and openness to the change that is part of life.  But, just as parasites and microbes defend themselves to survive, dysfunctional aspects of social life protect their survival through resistance to change and conformity.

The type of personality that gravitates toward psycho-spiritual inertia is the one in which the individual seeks comfort through avoiding conflicts and the narrowing of the conscience, at the same time becoming hyperactive—as if moving his energy from the essential to the accessory and from interiority to external issues.  In the social sphere this conjunction of loss of interiority and agitation is also manifest in a growing incapability for leisure.  Our modern secular world spins on itself, with higher noise levels, quicker and quicker, and people seem to be ever more addicted to distractions.  And that is how this leisure that we once expected the industrial age would give us, not only doesn't occur, but we are incapable of taking advantage of it because of our addiction to television and our horror in the face of emptiness.  In talking about Buenos Aires, Ernesto Sabato observed an alienating rush that seems to reign in all large cities: "In the streets, men and women hurriedly walk without looking at each other, wishing to comply with schedules that put their humanity in danger. There is no more room for the talks over coffee that were a distinctive characteristic of this city when ferocity and violence had not made it a megalopolis gone mad. Mothers used to be able to take their children to parks or to visit relatives. Can anything blossom at this speed? One of the objectives of this race seems to be productivity, but is it producing true fruits?

Mankind cannot stay human at this speed. If we live as automats, we will be annihilated. Serenity, a type of slowness, is as inseparable from the life of mankind as the seasons are from the life of the plants, or the birth of children."

The Jewish culture from which our culture was in part derived, considered leisure as its central commandment, in the understanding that there was a need to give time to the soul, have time to be alone and contact inner depth. Our need to get away from the world and the worldly has never been greater, and I think that it is precisely the secular, highly mundane character of our world that makes it imperative that we rediscover the sacred dimension of just being. I suspect that in our noisy, hyperactive world just understanding the value of resting our minds as a means to access spiritual peace could have a repairing effect.

But the place where we can find the specific antidote for the psycho-spiritual inertia that impregnates the modern secular world is in interiority, in attention placed on the individual experience and in an ethic of "working on oneself". We could expect that anything that supports the psycho-spiritual development of the individual will make us less passive with respect to the impulse of history and the strength of social habits and maybe nothing would be so useful to us as a form of education that takes into account self-knowledge and the optimization of interpersonal relationships. Education today is notoriously irrelevant to human development and this irrelevance could well be the most significant manifestation of the deadly ascidia alive in the modern world today: like a white elephant with the best of intentions, the educational system is hindering its own functioning through fossilization.

If we could completely understand how, in its obsolescence, it perpetuates our collective immaturity and we could decide to take a new path, it would contribute to our social evolution more than any other factor—besides the transformation of our economy.

### The Lie and the Illusion that Money Buys Happiness

If authoritarianism represents the domination of the paternal principle and the conformity that is represented as the childlike mentality of obedience, we could say that, both on an individual level and on a social level, these facets of life are complementary in the fact that they are deformations or falsifications of things that end up having a reconciling function, allowing the illusion that the designs of the authorities are benevolent and that conformity is the best alternative. For this reason, we could say that point 3 in the Enneagram corresponds to the function of a reconciling mother that, instead of defending the wishes and rights of the child, takes the side of the paternal authority.

When dealing with authoritarianism I have touched on the topic of the building of a fictitious reality, which corresponds with an analogous process in individual psychology: the level of our pathology (particularly so in the case of people whose capital sin is vanity) is the level on which we deceive ourselves and others by identifying with our idealized image of ourselves. No wonder spiritual traditions have determined that vanity is a "sin"—it takes us away from what is truly important, distracting us from charity or attention to our own development with the trivial or the ephemeral. And surely the same concept can be transposed to a social level where collectivity can lie by construction and perpetuate a false vision of what happens in the society. Just as we can say that the individual represses that which is not coherent with the self-image that he pretends to "sell", we could say that collectively the reality of what is happening in the world is ignored when it doesn't coincide with the implicit fiction transmitted by culture.

The following quote from Howard Fast seems to me to have the virtue of making us understand how much deceit has been associated with political control in all of history:

"Since you're a politician"—smiled Cicero—"perhaps you can tell me what a politician is".

"A deceiver"—responded Graco immediately.

"At least you're frank."

"It's my only virtue, one that is extremely valuable. In a politician people confuse it with honesty. You see: we live in a republic, which means there are a large number of people who have nothing and a small number who have a lot. Those who have a lot have to be defended and protected from those who have nothing. And not only that! Those who have a lot need to protect their property and for that reason those who have nothing must be willing to die for the property of people like you and I and our good host Anthony. As well, people like us have many slaves. These slaves don't like us. We should never think that slaves love their masters. They don't, and because of this slaves will not protect us against other slaves. So those who don't have slaves have to be willing to die so that we can have our slaves. Rome has a quarter of a million armed men. These soldiers must be willing to go to strange lands, to march until their feet are worn completely, to live in filth and misery, and to get blood on their hands and bleed themselves—so that we can be secure and live in comfort and increase our personal fortunes. When these troops went to fight against Spartacus they had less to defend than even the slaves did and nevertheless thousands died fighting against the slaves. We could go further. The countrymen that died fighting with the slaves were in the army in first place because they were run off of their lands by large land owners. The plantations that the slaves worked on turned them into miserable beings with no land and then they died to keep the plantations intact. We could be tempted to say, "reductio ad absurdum." So consider, dear Cicero, what is it that the brave Roman soldier would lose if the slaves were to win? They, in reality, need them desperately since there are not enough slaves to work the land adequately. The lands would be sufficient for everyone and our legionnaires would have what they most dreamed of, their plot of land and their home. And yet they march to destroy their own dream so that sixteen slaves can carry a fat old pig like me in a cushioned palanquin. Can you deny the truth of what I say?"

"I think that if what you're saying were to be said be a common man in the Forum we would crucify him."

"Cicero, Cicero,"—Graco laughs—"is that a threat? I'm too fat and heavy to be crucified. And why does hearing the truth make you so nervous? Is it necessary to lie to everyone? Is it necessary to believe our own lies?"

"It is as you say. Yet you simply leave out the key question—is each man the same or different from the other? There is an inconsistency in your little speech. You are supposing that men are similar like peas in a jar. I do not. There is an elite—a group of men who are superior. If the gods made them so or the circumstances made them take on roles, it is not something to be argued about. There are men made to govern, and they govern. And because others are like cattle, they behave like cattle. Look here: you present a theory. The difficulty is in the explanation. You speak of a society, but if the truth were as illogical as the picture you paint, the entire structure would collapse in a day. What you have not explained is what keeps this illogical puzzle functioning."

"Yes, I do"—Graco adds. "I keep it functioning."

"You? You alone?"

"Cicero, do you really think I'm an idiot? I have lived a long and dangerous life and I am yet on top. You asked me what a politician is. A politician is the cement in this crazy house. The patricians cannot run it alone. In the first place, they think as you do, and the Roman citizens don't like to be called cattle. They are not cattle—and you'll learn that someday. In second place, the patricians know nothing about the citizens. If left alone the structure would collapse in one day. That is why they come to people like me. They wouldn't be able to live without people like me. We rationalize the irrational. We convince people that the greatest objective in life is to die for the rich. We convince the rich that they must give up part of their fortune to support the rest of the people. We are like magicians. We create an illusion and the illusion is foolproof. We tell the people—"You have the power. Your vote is the source of the strength and glory of Rome. You are the only free people in the world. There is nothing more precious than your freedom, nothing more admirable than your civilization. And you control it all: you are the power." They then vote for our candidates. They weep our defeats. They are joyful for our victories. And they feel proud and superior because they aren't slaves. It doesn't matter how low they are. It doesn't matter if they sleep in the street, if they sit in public seats in the arena all day, if their newborns are killed, if the live on charity and never raise a hand to work from birth to death; the important thing is that they aren't slaves. They are shit, but each time they see a slave, their egos rise up and they feel full of pride and power. Then they know that they are Roman citizens and that the entire world is envious of them. And this is my art, Cicero. Never put down or denigrate a politician."

(Extract from *Spartacus* by Howard Fast, 1951)

The fundamental issue in the psychology of vanity (equal to what the North American sociologist David Riesman called "the personality turned toward the environment"[7]) is the confusion between the intrinsic value of people or things and an extrinsic or market value determined by the appreciation of others; and, wishing to underline the importance of this distortion, Erich Fromm, some five decades ago, spoke of a "mercantile orientation" of the personality. By this he wasn't talking literally about people interested in business, as we might think, but about people who are exaggeratedly motivated by success, who occupy themselves excessively with caring for and selling their image. It is not strange that

---

[7] In his book *The Lonely Crowd* he classifies people as traditionalists, autonomous and "other directed"—influenced by the opinions of the environment.

the American culture, where this type of personality abounds, is characterized by the domination of the motivational power of gain and ever-present propaganda. And although, in contrast with military power, economic power is held in transnational corporations more than in sovereign states, it cannot be denied that it has been the military domination of the USA that has served the interest of global capitalism, allowing the motivational power of gain to reach the supremacy it has today, more than ever in history. I quote Parenti again:

"From 1977 to 1993 the top 1% multiplied their earnings by 100. Salaries and benefits of corporation executives went from 35 times the average salary of a blue-collar worker to almost 150 times. Today the top 1% of the population receives as much in earnings (after taxes) as the bottom 40%." And as an interpretation, he concludes: "The purpose of ruling interests is to keep society and the entire world open to a maximum of earnings, independently of human and environmental costs. The true burden of society is not the poor but the incorporated rich. We just cannot afford them anymore."

While the world gets richer, poverty becomes more notorious[8] and it becomes more obvious that we have a

---

[8]Bertrand Schneider says in his book *The Scandal and the Shame of Poverty and Underdevelopment: Report for the Club of Rome:*

"(...) new forms of control of the world economy and of submitting peoples are being developed, planned by the large multinationals, the most powerful nations in the world, and certain international organisms. The distance between North and South grows greater and greater. Only a few control science and technology. Economic, financial, commercial, technological, political and military power is concentrated and centralized in very few hands.

"Faced by these changes, a large number of the men and women that inhabit Earth contemplate their present and their immediate future with little hope. Poverty and hunger in the world have increased. The majority of the population has been excluded from making the decisions that affect their lives and their future. The access to basic needs has decreased: property, land, the use of goods, technical advances, health and education.

problem with money. The governments and politics of today are occupied mainly with money and it is true that many believe that it is the economic issues that we must deal with in order to have a better world. Poverty is not only a cause of suffering for those who are affected by hunger and lack of housing, but also a serious interference in social functions like raising children and education—which in turn contributes to perpetuating social and individual underdevelopment. However, excessive worry about the economic problem may be part of the problem itself, and it seems improbable to me that we could solve it without attending to the internal or psychological aspect, that involves envy, injustice and impotence in the face of supposedly ineluctable market laws. We are slaves of the market only in as much as we choose to exclude from our consideration other values that aren't gain and economy; meaning as we choose to give priority to gain over finding the sense of our lives and cultivating healthy human relations.

Now that money is more powerful than the sovereign states with their armies and the small percentage of those that control more than half of the riches in the world have shown no interest in placing their power at the service of human values and Christian precepts, how can we conceive evolutive change?

If it is true that we cannot "serve two masters" there will have to be a time when we choose to subordinate "Mamon"[9] to something larger; a time when we understand

---

(Schneider, cont.) "Models of political, economic and socio-cultural organization have been imposed that are destined to break the culture of communities and create absolute dependency on and servitude to the strong, in the hope of an uncertain future. The United Nations Report, "Human Development 1994", confirms that, while the difference between the top 20% in the world and the poorest people was 30 to 1 in 1960, in 1994 this proportion had risen to 60 to 1. (...)"

[9] In modern Bibles it is translated as "money." In older ones it's personified.

that it is not good business to attend exclusively to business; a time when we are prepared to abandon our passivity with respect to the "law of supply and demand." In the name of this law and of "free enterprise" we have allowed humanity to be trampled, but we are not so impotent or irresponsible as the economists want us to think when they use the concept of the "homo economicus" that only buys and sells. I don't doubt that Marx was right in his conviction that we need to transcend the straitjacket of capitalism, that he interpreted as the subordination of life (in its work aspect) to death (capital, as belonging to the world of objects). In view of this, I think it is a disgrace that the happy event of the failure of Stalinism made Marx fall into forgotten-ness and made his reputation disappear among academics: this is equivalent to "throwing the baby out with the bath water"[10]. Certainly Marx made many mistakes and what the Soviet Union did in his name was atrocious, but we should not use the failure of the soviet system as a pro-capitalist argument—particularly when the capitalistic crisis represents a challenge for our capacity to survive.

I don't know how we would ever be able to end the enormous inequality that exists in the distribution of riches in the world, because money buys power and the powerful people in the world have little interest in giving it up. In one of his books, Hillaire Belloc predicted that from the economic and political facts of his time (during the first half of the 20th century) could be deduced a growing enslaving of the world, and that seems to be happening. I suspect that, like in check mate, we are condemned to impotence, since the forces of darkness are greater than those of light, but there is something that we can do so that the situation is different for the generation that follows ours: educate children and young people today in such a way that they will later be healthy and wise beings who can chose to create a better world.

---

[10]Expression that alludes to how sometimes, by invalidating a detail, the essential part of a thought is set aside.

## *Beyond the Holy Wars, the Search for Self-Realization*

If the way out depends on a combination of efforts like pacifism, the fight for justice, or a representative democracy, can we be optimistic? Many think we cannot, and naturally the defenders of the system prefer that we abandon all hope of changing it.

As in the individual's holy war against his ego, effort is needed, but our sense of reality makes enthusiasm difficult, since the alliance of neoliberalism with technology is rapidly making the world into a market of products and work, delegitimizing all values. And in an environment in which the individual, more and more at the mercy of the market, has less and less options, remedies like those I have proposed become weak.

In previous ages, it was religion that legitimized moral values, but secularization of the system is quickly making it into a fairy tale that only primitive people would be presumed to believe. Besides, the logically resulting death of ideals not only reached into religion but into culture in general:   the living transmission of humanity in which ideals or values are naturally inserted.

This is why it is hopeful to consider the proposal that the social pathologies we have examined in this chapter are merely symptoms of a deeper problem whose solution has not yet been contemplated, and it is also hopeful that the appropriate solution to the diagnosis of a "patriarchal disease" holds more the promotion of development than a series of crusades.   That this diagnosis points to a psychological imbalance implies that individual development holds political potential.

So the sins, deviations or pathologies need to be corrected in the individual through comprehension and the desire for purification, and it is also true that said defects show a certain limitation of the conscience, a lack of experience and underdevelopment of certain capacities. The individual, then, not only needs to fight a holy war against his ego, but also to cultivate aspects of himself that are underdeveloped, which involves the development of the corresponding virtues.

Analogically it seems to me that on a social scale it is not enough to fight our evils and that it is time that we tried to build up what we lack: the fact that we are behind in our development toward being complete beings, and especially the development of those aspects of our mind that in the patriarchal world have been eclipsed by the preponderance of the authoritarian intellect:    the wise and deep-seated spontaneity of our instinctive being and our archaic capacity to establish loving relationships.   Sustaining that our illness is the patriarchal condition of our mind could seem to be very different from what is proposed in current theories in vogue in the academic world —but in reality they are not so different. Saying that our problem consists of a hegemony of the "father" aspect of our nature over the maternal and filial aspects (whether in interpersonal relationships in the family or in intra-psychic life) is not very different from the Freudian vision of a "superego" that becomes the owner and overseer of instinctive life.   In reality the Freudian vision of neurosis as the result of ever-changing instincts is no other than the description of an inner tyrant derived from the internalization of the authority of the father in society—except that Freud, in spite of his revolutionary spirit, succumbed sufficiently to the conservative and patriarchal spirit of his time and believed more in the kindness of civilization than in the kindness of human instinctiveness.

Whether we talk about a "father" principle or a sub-personality or a superego (and in reality the Freudian "superego" has been transformed today into the "parent" of Erick Berne) the therapeutic business in the post-Freudian world has greatly consisted of a process of freeing instinctiveness and therefore an implicit reintegration of our reptilian brain and of our aspect as a simple creature, sometimes referred to in contemporary therapy as the "inner child".   This gives us hope and any wise government today should recognize the political potential of psychotherapy in the fundamental sense of the word—beyond its Machiavellic form.

### Reverence for Childhood, Decriminalization of Pleasure and Recovery of Instinctiveness

I will begin with the relegation of the primitive, instinctive or animal aspect of our nature, since modern psychotherapy has attended to this and contributed to the clarity we have now.

Koestler and Toynbee thought, some decades ago, that when we became man at the dawn of our prehistorical age we were expelled from the paradise that consisted in natural order, that when we decided to follow our reason more than our instincts, a disconnection between our instinctive brain and our human brain—the neocortex—was produced, which would come to be our greatest tragedy.

Although I am in agreement as to the tragedy that is our intra-psychic disconnection, I do not think that it should be interpreted as intrinsic to the biological evolution of our brain. We know today that the oppression that the authority of the superego exerts on our instinctive regulation represents the result of learning, and where there is learning there is the possibility of re-education—or of un-learning.

A patriarchal world, by definition, entails the preponderance of a father figure in the family system, but the internal imbalance that interests us here is caused by the preponderance of the neocortex, intellectually specialized, over our "mammalian brain" or middle brain, that is our relational organ, and over our instinctive or reptilian brain. And I add that even though we have had a feminist movement and even though the voice of youth made itself heard in the 60's, we have not had, to date, a children's liberation movement—a "children's lib." It is difficult to conceive that a movement like this would ever come about because the needs and perceptions of children are the ones that are most repressed in the home and because children are dependent and have no power, whereas adults, in general, have less capacity to be parents than they think and the power they exert is an

overcompensation for a sensation of incompetence as well as a
vaguely perceived moral inadequacy. Our inner child (in all
of us) has been so invalidated and frustrated that an effective
psychological cure requires realizing what has been done to us
—through emotional memories (and catharsis) of the pain we
went through and also through the consciousness of early rage.
And this is not enough if we are going to be complete human
beings again: our inner child has to be brought back to life.
But this is still not enough, because if we consider that in each
of us there are three sub-personalities (an echo of our parents
and our inner child) we have to take into account that the inner
child scarcely has had a voice in our inner family policies, so
we not only have to reestablish life for the inner child and free
him but welcome him so that he has a voice and a vote in the
inner dialog. For those who today follow a spiritual path,
many, without a doubt, feel great devotion toward a divine
being with fatherly characteristics, and some hold a sense of
the sacredness of life or "Mother Earth" or the Universe, but it
seems to me that not many among the seekers have the
necessary recognition or appreciation for the divine inner
child, and less even for the simplicity of our universal inner
new born. But I do not believe that enlightenment will be
possible without returning to the sacredness of this
consciousness that is simple beyond all contents that preceded
our intellectual development, forming the underlying reality to
our notion of a subject of the conscience. Today we tend to
believe that we begin as "nobodies" and then evolve as nature
evolves through a growing complexity, but this is only one
aspect of things, since in healthy development complexity
does not eliminate simplicity, only with the deterioration of
consciousness do the ramifications that occur in our mind
forget the trunk of the tree of life, which, of course, interferes
in the ability of the branches to bear fruit. If biological
evolution brings greater complexity, psycho-spiritual
evolution also brings the progressive penetration of
complexity in individual consciousness, which is very simple,
aconceptual, basic and as archaic as that original face that Zen
teaches us that we had before our parents were born.

I have announced this digression with respect to the filial aspect of our nature by talking about revering childhood and not only love, as it seems to me that this shade of love is the one that most needs to be exalted in compensation for the implicit indifference toward children that is usually accompanied by paternalism and maternalism, both protectionist and controlling. We are in need of the attitude that characterizes the archetypical situation of the adoration of the Christ Child by the Three Wise Men, which has so inspired great artists, but that barely inspires parents today to be humble when faced with their children's consciousness. The initiative of Laura Huxley seems exceptional to me. With Piero Ferrucci, she has founded an organization that has been baptized "Children, Our Supreme Investment." In a brief article ironically titled "Big Business as Educators of the Divine Child", this author informs us that in the USA an adolescent gives birth every minute, each day 2,756 children drop out of school, 5,753 children are arrested and there are 8,470 reports of abuse or negligence. In the same country, every two hours a child is the victim of homicide (and the punishment for the crime is less that in the murder of an adult) and each four hours a child commits suicide. To me, these statistics validate the theory of Raskowsky, Argentinean psychoanalyst, who decades ago declared that infanticide impulses were more universal than the parricide impulses so sensationally emphasized by Freud, and that the generalized aggression towards parents is just the consequence of the destructiveness, also generalized but less recognized, of parents toward children.

But the article by Laura Huxley is not about intra-family relations but, as the title announces, a social phenomenon: the competition established between big companies and parents and educators when these companies are interested in children as future consumers. For example, she writes:

"Yes, children are our most important investment, but they are also investments for promoters of nicotine. Every day in the USA 3,000 young people begin a habit of smoking…"

"Yes, children are our most important investment, but they are also investments for the powerful alcohol conglomerate. In 1996 the total amount spent in alcoholic consumption by young people was 52.8 billion dollars."

And further on: "Parents! You are the target of what Ralph Nader has called predatory businesses". And, echoing Nader's concept that "companies are electronic abusers of children", she proposes, "There is a historically unprecedented war going on between parents and business. It is a battle for the minds, bodies, time and space of millions of children and the world they will grow up in."

Naturally, the interference in childhood develop-ment through the inhibition of play, premature disciplinarian schooling, and the bombarding of TV finally silences the divine child in each of us. More than a century ago, Nietzsche criticized Christianity for its sins against the land and proclaimed that only the Dionysian spirit would be able to remedy our collective situation. What did he mean? That our civilization is painfully constricted, over-controlled, excessively subject to our limited ideals and our corresponding sense of what should be. The Dionysian spirit, symbolized by the spirit of wine, indicates our disposition to die to ourselves in an act of surrender, going beyond limits, dissolving our consciousness in a larger field. Of course, Christian mystics have been acquainted with surrender to the point of meeting a type of death in the divine, but in spite of wine and Church, with its theologians, the Church has not been supportive of its own mystics, at least while they were alive. And not only the Church but the patriarchal culture it is inserted into needs a greater Dionysian spirit because Dionysius, the marginal god of the Greeks, breaks with forms in his deep alliance with life as it is and as it wishes to be. I am convinced that the initiates to the ancient mysteries knew the inseparability between Apollo and Dionysius well, the incarnation of apparently contradictory qualities: lucidity and drunkenness, domination and surrender, balance and enthusiasm. But we can assuredly say that in the Christian world there has never existed a case of comparable comparison or comparable realization because, if there had been, the image of Dionysius would not have been used to characterize the devil. It is not sufficient for us to have the Apollonian and patriarchal qualities of lucidity, dominion and detachment without the corresponding Dionysian and matristic capacities of surrender to the mysteries of the flow of life.

The freeing of our inner child requires that we have an attitude that is very different from the one that can be achieved through discipline. It requires precisely the relaxation of all discipline and the cultivation of innocent inner freedom.

We need discipline, we need austerity, and we also need a quality that I have no better name for than "organismic trust": trust in our impulses, trust in the wisdom of our spontaneity and trust in pleasure as a compass for our instinctive self. I think that, just as the divine manifests itself in our conscience with the triple image of father, mother and child, we can only find plenitude through the harmonic development of these components of our humanity and our thirst for transcendence without maternal love or without the freedom of the child is only compatible with pale devotion. On the other hand, for a person in whom the "mother" aspect is excessively dominant, the metaphysical insight or wisdom that is characteristic of a complete spiritual experience will be very difficult. And in a person in whom the "child" principle is dominant it is difficult to conceive reaching plenitude because of the maturity of love and wisdom that is lacking.

Without opening up to the instinctive self that is intrinsic to our earthly nature—as human beings who are also animals—I believe it is difficult to reach happiness or a healthy society and I wonder if it is not precisely the fact that spiritual stagnation persists in spite of the richness of diverse traditional paths because the inner child in our nature has no space or defender in this world. This defender would understand his mission as breaking the dam that impoverishes us through the alienation of our instinctive nature with all its normal appetites, its search for pleasure and avoidance of pain: a dam made of self-hate that confuses the instinctual with the world of neurotic motivations. I believe the ancient

Babylonians and Egyptians knew very well that the realization of the divine in humankind is directly related to the sanctification of the inner animal, which is shown through their representations of divinities with animal heads and other characteristics. Of course, shamans have always understood this from finding themselves, for example, before the spirit of the eagle upon entering their path.

### The Recovery of the "Maternal Instinct" and the Capacity for Empathetic and Solidary Bonds

From Freud on, therapists have understood pathologies in terms of an inner barrier in the mind that is created by the operation of defense mechanisms that filter experiences, a type of artificial membrane that our socialization has provoked in us between our unconscious and conscious mind. But the idea of a three-part brain subject to patriarchal domination suggests a conception of pathology in terms of two barriers, since we are talking about the structure of three-brained beings. It is not only a barrier between consciousness and the unconscious. In an alternative theoretical frame we can consider two intra-psychic borders or dikes that isolate our insular psychic world under the empire of reason: a border between the world of reason and the instinctive world and another where the neocortex and the middle brain meet, meaning, between reason and affectivity (with its respective love). And is it not true that the critical condition of mankind is specifically caused by a deficit in the capacity to love? If we have alienated our inner reptile we have also alienated our inner mammal, and due to the supremacy of reason, we have put the considerations of affections aside in our lives.

Nietzsche was surely right when he said that Christian civilization needed to return to Dionysius, as he was also right in his understanding of the falseness in what is said to be Christian love or compassion, and it is understandable that he became bitterly cynical and believed that compassion was always a trap or lie. But I think that just as the enlightenment of Zarathustra lacked a mother figure, Nietzsche did not have the experience of a loving partner in his life.

Even though we lack spontaneity and the freeing of our desires in the therapeutic process geared toward loving, the fact that the critical condition of humankind points specifically to a deficit in love tells us that education for love is just as important as education for spontaneity.

A consequence of the supremacy of reason has been the setting aside of considerations of the affective domain and this aspect of our dehumanization is ever more present. It is enough to remember and compare our family life experience with what our ancestors have told us.

In our technocratic world, affective and vital needs are reduced to nothing when faced with macro-economic considerations. It is as if the "mother" principle were sufficiently absent from our culture so that children are raised in an atmosphere deprived of empathy, love and attention to the affective needs of each moment.

Affective needs of children are betrayed at every turn and Joseph Chilton Pierce, in his books *The Magical Child* and *Evolution's End,* has eloquently explained the way in which the patriarchy—technocratic, authoritarian and anti-maternal—treats our children beginning in the delivery room, contributing to the atrophy of the loving capacity in the human race.

The unnecessary acceleration of births because of scheduling convenience and anesthesia, interfering with the conscious transition of newborns into their new atmosphere, together with the premature cutting of the umbilical cord, are habitual practices that were, until recently, considered harmless but that today are known to be catastrophic. This is proven by the findings, some years ago, that the reflex the baby has to follow his mother's face with his eyes and respond to her smile—observed in the western world at about six months of age—is present in Africans from the first day of life[11]. The reason for the discrepancy is not genetic, but can be

---

[11]Cited by J. C. Pearce in *Evolution's End.*

explained by the long recovery that our babies must go through after the traumatic shock of "technological births." Even the classic "spanking" that is given to babies, with the supposed intention of helping them expel mucous that does not allow them to breathe, has been shown to be useless: an act of implicit aggression inspired by a spirit similar to the cruel initiation rites of warriors. It is as if the doctor is saying to the newborn; "Grow up boy, and breathe deeply in spite of the shock that me hitting you implies."

I have been especially impressed by something from among the facts that Chilton Pearce talks about and that is dramatic proof that natural births are convenient, no matter what uninterested authorities say:

In his book *Evolution's End*, the author we have mentioned talks about how in 1979 the California government financed the first scientific study on the fundamental causes of crime and violence. The report that came out three years later concluded that the main cause of the growing epidemic of violence in the United States had been the violence perpetuated against newborns and their mothers during birth. He goes on to give the bad news of the sad deterioration of the Afro-American community because of "assimilation into the technocratic world":

"In the South, where I come from, before World War II the black community attended to their births through their own network of mid-wives and the principal characteristic of these black communities was solidarity. They took care of their people and used extended families—a main ingredient in all true societies. They took care of each other, not only spurred on by the need to survive, but also spontaneously because of their capacity to establish bonds that were ensured by home births. I have witnessed the destruction of the power of the extended family in the poor black communities—their strength through centuries of oppression—by simply moving their births from the hands of midwives to charity hospitals where the new mothers receive truly atrocious treatment. Today many of those mothers are single teenagers virtually with no family or support system, without education, with no understanding of motherhood, not to mention the ever-present influence of drugs, alcohol and AIDS.  The situation is getting worse at an alarming rate.

"Many of these adolescents want to have a baby and say that they got pregnant in order to have someone to love and who loves them: a natural instinct.  They think that maternity will give them self-esteem in a world that despises them.  They have no idea what they will face when they leave the hospital, when they discover the battle they will have with the children that they dreamed of as sources of love.  In previous years black mothers were model mothers, like Mary Ainsworth and Marcelle Geber learned in old Uganda.  This is no longer true in the United States."

Especially catastrophic is the lack of recognition of the early mother-child bond, which requires a maximum of bodily contact between mother and child.  Although we are no longer in the elegant setting of France in the 19th century, when mothers gave their children over to wet nurses so that their daily lives would not be interfered in, we would do well to give our children the loving and sensitive treatment common in African and Pre-Colombian cultures.[12]

We know, through Harlow's studies with macaques half a century ago, that females that have been deprived of adequate maternity "do not know how to be good mothers" when the time comes for them to feed their own offspring.  Everything indicates, as well, that the human capacity for nutrition and attending to the needs of others requires the experience of good mothering in order to develop.  It seems that the maternal function is learned and is passed down through generations.

To the interference in the establishment of the important bond between mother and child, we can add later interferences that are familiar to us:  the mother leaves the home because of the need to work, for example, and the lack of bonding because of "psycho-dynamical" complications:

---

[12]Jean Liedlow develops this topic in her book *The Continuum Concept*.

typically, conflicts between the mother and the father that cause the child to take sides, and when antagonism with the father is internalized, its corresponding devaluation causes the inner mother to be alienated or deprived of existence.

Moving from home to school, the betrayal of the mother is accented and begins with premature schooling. A sign of exactly how patriarchal traditional education is that (in spite of our natural association of the vocation of teachers with the maternal spirit) uncountable educational proposals systematically leave out the word love. Even when the discussion takes into account the importance of interpersonal education and the development of a civic attitude, it seems as though words like "compassion" and "love" are implicitly taboo. To me this is a reflection of the scientific and rationalist empire that is characteristic of the patriarchal culture: the topic of love is considered too romantic, perhaps adequate for art but not for a "serious conversation." This tells me that even after decades of feminism during which much advance has been made in the area of women's rights in the labor world and in the political world, not much has been achieved in the balance between masculine and feminine *values*. It is very possible that we try to solve issues that have to do with injustice because of gender by giving power to women without touching on the fundamental issue, which is the preference of power over love.

Of course, the inclusion of women in positions of power could be expected to lead, over time, to policies that take into account the dictates of the heart along with the dictates of reason, but we still live in times in which the exploitation of the Earth and of people is largely greater than their cultivation, in that competition is much greater than cooperation, and power is greater than love. Even when we are so interested in ecology and speak against the violation of the Earth, we do it in terms of economic considerations and not in terms of a healthy sense of belonging to the ecosphere and to the ecosystem as our noble, more integral, "primitive" ancestors did.

### And What of the Spirit?

It is not enough to become harmonious, healthy and loving three-brained beings—capable of joyful peace: it is also about becoming spiritual beings—which implies that, beyond educating the body to work, the heart to live in relationships, and the mind for the knowledge of the universe, we must have an education that favors the contemplative disposition of the mind, and not only the intellectual and psychological aspects.

Above and beyond learning to be and learning to live with others, even beyond learning to learn, it is important to learn to be—in order to finally get to the divine root of consciousness through the mystery of emptiness. But since my own pedagogical exploration of the experience of being, manifest in the "SAT Process," will be the object of the second part of this book, I can end this small chapter here. I only want to end my digressions by suggesting that what Totila Albert called "The Religion of the Three" is intrinsically spiritual—since the Spirit is precisely the uniting force in the diversity among areas of experience of our inner persons—and at the same time "a neutral nothingness" or transparency in whose embrace our three inner parts can function in a unified and harmonious way.

### Education as the Most Promising Route of Escape

Throughout my life's work—at least during the last three decades—I held an implicit supposition: that by doing what I know how to do best—helping people to grow and heal—I was contributing to the life of society. In a certain sense I was correct, since society is made up of individuals, but I think I may have been wrong in supposing that by helping in the development of consciousness of a few I was also helping the world to change.

Among those who culture deprives of complete development only some suffer and their suffering is like a call to plenitude, a demand for suspected health. No wonder Jung spoke of a "sacred neurosis" and no wonder the ancient ones venerated those they deemed crazy, since those who do not suffer are like people who have gone through the amputation of a limb and don't realize what has happened to them, people alienated and not even conscious of their alienation. Just like the shamans of archaic cultures whose suffering only ceased when they learned to cure the disease (something the profane see as mysterious) that the pain revealed to them, the seekers of today suffer from the limitation of the world and aspire to the return to the "paradise lost" of the original unified consciousness. And in view of the relevance of personal development in the social change that we desire, as well as in view of the maturity that psychotherapy achieved in the last century, the enthusiasm that accompanied the therapeutic boom of the "revolution of the consciousness" seems justified.

My implicit faith in helping the development of the consciousness of "aspiring shamans" as a new way of helping the world went together with the notion that the progress in consciousness would be inevitably contagious and I implicitly held onto the hope in what has been referred to as the phenomenon of the hundredth monkey. Particularly, since I found out about the discovery of this phenomenon some decades ago, I trusted that when a certain critical mass of people in the world evolved enough, there would be a contagion of consciousness that would affect the evolution of the whole world.

"The phenomenon of the hundredth monkey" refers to an event observed by anthropologists some decades ago on the coasts of some island in the Pacific: although the monkeys had eaten certain tubers for an extremely long time, some of them discovered that they could wash the tubers in sea water, and the discovery was contagious. In other words: washing the tubers became a cultural element in the life of these animals, transmitted by imitation and learning. What was unusual, however—and what defied the usual scientific explanations and invoked Rupert Sheldrake's hypothesis of morphogenetic fields[13], was when the act of washing the

---

[13]Sheldrake, Rupert: *A New Science of Life: The Hypothesis of Formative Causation,* Kairos, Barcelona 1990.

tubers became generalized and the monkeys on nearby islands, that had no contact with the monkeys that had learned the new conduct, began to do the same thing. It was as though the group consciousness of the monkeys reached a certain limit allowing transmission in a rather unknown way, "parapsychologically."

In a comparable manner, I thought it would be enough for an adequate number of people to reach a high level of development of consciousness for that to cause generalization through contagion. At the beginning of the 60s it was easy to think that the new spiritual and therapeutic fermentation—a true rebirth—would over time affect the entire world. Nevertheless, the counterrevolution of the 80s put an end to what seemed to be a glorious summer in our cultural history, and the countryside turned to autumn. The more apparent the loss of spiritual and cultural values becomes, the more it seems to me that what could be called the post-humanistic movement (residual of that "new age" that was the echo of the Freudian and Marxist revolutions) is an issue for minorities.

When, in the 60s, we were "learning to wash our potatoes" it seemed that soon the entire world would throw itself into the magical journey that is the path to transformation. Today it seems to me that each of the new shamans finds himself in a situation similar to that of Jonathan Livingston Seagull: a solitary soul faced by a multitude that is only interested in surviving the best way they can. (Whoever has read the fable will remember how Jonathan Livingston Seagull was interested in flying higher than the horizon, while other gulls preferred to flit around the dock near the abundant remains of city food).

There can be many seekers in the world, but the world is so big and so densely populated with sleep walkers, unconscious of the fact that their development has been detained, that the metaphor of Jonathan Livingston Seagull in the book by Richard Bach is still applicable and the march of collective events suggests that the world government is impermeable to spiritual consciousness and the dictates of wisdom and love. I very much doubt, at least, that the consciousness of our subpopulation of seekers is on the verge of reaching the critical mass required to change the direction of the world. And as time passes it seems to me that my own work essentially attracts a minority of intuitive seekers that are interested in more than their own well-being. The thing that most attracts attention, forty years after the glorious awakening of the "human potential movement," is how the world moves in a way that is absolutely separate from the consciousness that seemed triumphant in the then utopian enthusiasm.

We are moving dizzily toward a world submitted to an empire made up of a network of multinational companies in which love is impotent when faced with the power of money and the thirst for gain. The consequences are the bleeding of the meek, the victimizing of the poor and the bombing of the innocent. To complicate matters even further, the progressive awareness of the public of the criminal history of the Church together with current spiritual impoverishment has made us untrusting and cynical toward any form of spirituality—therefore barely receptive of any influence that could help us.

During my visit to Chile in January of this year (2001) I was invited to participate in a meeting of the Latin American Economic Commission (CEPAL), a branch of the United Nations in which an original proposal was being considered: that in the UN not only should the heads of State be gathered, but also representatives of spiritual traditions. I was surprised and moved during the conference when the representative of the World Bank of Geneva—Mr. CEFIR—spoke of the abyss that exists today between economy and spirituality. I would have never imagined such a declaration by a person in his position, and I felt hopeful to hear that, in his opinion, the most important challenge in our times would be to build a bridge between these two worlds in order to achieve a human economy.

Stimulated by this declaration came the idea to reunite a fistful of those people who have the largest fortunes in the world and to invite them—along with spiritually developed people like the Dalai Lama and perhaps representatives of other alternative positions (like Hazel Henderson, Macneff or Cavanaugh)—to dream together; dream of what a fair and healthy economy would be like. If people who are at the center of the system, like this man, have begun to think this way, a "revolution from the inside" becomes conceivable, and the moment will have come to say "capitalists of the world unite"—no longer as accomplices, but as pioneers in transformation. My experience as a therapist tells me that the liberation of the individual requires a type of abdication by the ego that allows the freedom of the true self, and the indication of spiritual consciousness in the interstitial area of the monetary system suggests that there are seeds of change precisely there.

So, the growing concentration of capital in the world would be hopeful if it weren't for the patriarchal system in agony that is taking its toll on lives and values and destroying the environment. With the implacable wave of destruction that the world is immersed in and the very slight possibility of generating peace, justice, democracy and other values in civic life, it would be logical to think that education would be a lifesaver for a ship that is sinking.

The result is that education, so badly paid and so devalued, promises today what traditional religions, technology or the therapeutic movement can no longer promise. Except that, for this potential to be expressed, our current education (which up to now has only been a means of socialization through which a sick culture perpetuates itself) must become something much different.

It is necessary for education to stop being a patriarchal institution and move toward the phenomenon of balanced development of our "three inner persons." We need the balance of our three brains and the balance of our thinking, our feeling, and our doing. In view of the urgency of this need, the many proposals that exist today in the educational world seem to me to be dangerously limited and the stimulus of the UNESCO has been barely more effective than that of the UN Safety Council. Nevertheless, I think that we have the human resources and the knowledge needed to transform education and I hope that this book, with the good news of a new powerful resource, will make a difference. Throughout its chapters I describe the work I've been doing for many years with seekers, therapists, psychologists in formation and educators in a program that has sometimes been described as a school of love and others as a process of humanization. It is a work that has evolved almost by itself, through me, and when I contemplate its current level of effectiveness I realize that I have discovered something that is truly useful for the public, since the application in education of this same series of experiences that has elevated the level of life and capabilities of diverse professionals promises to help not only teachers in the future but the emerging society in its entirety.

## 4.  An Education for Personal and Social Evolution

*"Correct answers", specialization, standardization, narrow competence, avid acquisition, aggression, detachment. Without them it seems to us that the social machine would not be able to function. We should not accuse schools of cruelty when they are only complying with what society has asked them for. But the reason we need radical reform in education is that the demands that society makes have been changing radically. There is no doubt that the human characteristics that we promote today will one day no longer be functional. They have already become inappropriate and destructive. If education stays the way it has been, humanity will end up destroying itself sooner or later."*

G. Leonard, Op. cit.

The topic has been announced and it is practically a thesis: it is time that we had education for human development. This implies the implicit conviction that without education for human development, it will be difficult for us to have a better society.

Up to now, we have lived a long history of noble proposals and bloody revolutions for social change that have not taken into account individual change, and it seems to be time for us to understand that if we want a different society, we have to be more complete human beings: we cannot build something like this without the appropriate elements.

This is a topic that I have been interested in for many years, an interest that was born as I began to suspect the political value of the education of the individual and, of course, I use the term "political" in the larger sense of the word, alluding to public good and not to the Machiavellian politics of power. I thought then that understanding the potential of education for social evolution would be an easy thing to transmit to receptive people in the educational system, who in turn could do what was needed to make education more relevant to change. But it has been some fifteen years now, during which I've realized that something very strange is taking place in education: it is a very well-intentioned institution, an area where in all countries participants talk continually about possible reform and particularly about complementary and alternative curriculum, they hold conferences, they invest a lot of money, and nothing fundamental changes. The dominating factor is an enormous institutional inertia.

And to me, this seems tragic, just like it seems tragic to me also that among all the evils in the world, this one is almost invisible. I think that human development is fundamental, not only to build a viable society, but also to achieve individual happiness, since I do not believe we are in this world just to survive, and I think that it would behoove us to think more about our planet as a type of purgatory that we have come to in order to do inner work: cultivate our spirits and go away being better than when we arrived.

Even a staunch materialist or a doctrinarian agnostic will acknowledge that "man does not live on bread alone". But how is it possible that after millenniums of reflecting on the destiny of mankind, on the happiness that comes from virtue and the perfectibility of our condition, there is still, in the civilized world, an institution that calls itself "educational" but that only attends to things that are relatively insignificant? It is evident that instead of helping people to be good people so that we have a good world, this institution occupies itself with teaching subjects that, supposedly, will serve us in our professional lives or that, supposedly, will serve us in the education of certain aspects of our minds, in detriment to other aspects. More than anything else, current education helps us pass exams and achieve a privileged spot in the job market, and thus it is exact to say that the social organ that should be watching out for human development is occupied in irrelevances, casting aside its function—just when human development has become extremely urgent given the current state of the world.

Today we hear about a crisis in education. By why are people talking about a crisis? It is because young students do not want the education that is being offered. And since this is fundamentally what causes the institution to speak of a crisis, we could say that what is taking place is a marketing crisis, interpreted very unilaterally and only half understood.

We mainly blame the youth. The thought is: "We are in crisis because young people are no longer interested in their studies like they used to be," "young people are not as serious as in other times," "young people take drugs and so they are incapable of listening to serious people who bring such important subjects into the classroom." And no one thinks that maybe the situation is the opposite: it may be that young people are acquiring a more awakened conscious than the teachers that have been programmed for traditional teaching, and that young people only need brief contact with school to realize they are not interested in it. Even the effect of drugs (which is blamed so much in the United States and, through the echo of North American politics, in the rest of the world) has been the opening for existential questions, giving young people a sense that there are many things in life that are urgent and that the classroom calls irrelevant. Existential issues are systematically drowned out by a situation that lacks in human contact, the dialog that deals with what is happening in the students' minds, families and environment is ignored while they are expected to sit quietly at desks and are trained in obedience. In relation, currently it has been proven that the inhibition of the ludic impulse causes considerable brain damage, since there are synapses that are specifically stimulated by play and are then lost. I think that going to school today is like eating sand—eating something that is not nutritional—when we know by intuition that there is something that would be relevant, and it is criminal to make people waste energy and years of life in the supposition that this is what they need. What is needed is different: something that aids in human development.

Human development is much more than information and, above all, much more than the type of information that now occupies educators, which does not even apply to life, but, as I said, applies to receiving a paper that says that a person has the right to pass to the next level of studies. By saying this I do not wish to underestimate the evaluation of learning or set aside the process of selection in universities or in the job market. I only wish to point out the aberration that education has become since learning has been taken on more from the vantage point of good or bad grades than from that of an interest in learning.

It is very difficult to change anything in education, and in contrast to other times in which I felt optimistic, I am beginning to think that just as we have heard of an industrial military complex in which conscious violence and the tyranny that money imposes are confused, perhaps we should ask ourselves if education, knowingly or not, is the secret weapon of this oppressive system: a system serving as an accomplice to the economic system, that instead of helping human consciousness and the balance of society, serves to perpetuate the status quo[1] and at the same time, hypocritically, ignorance (in the deepest meaning of the word, not related to alphabetization, but to understanding what happens to us and around us). The person who understands what is happening cannot help but to be moved and to feel the implicit tragedy in the dysfunction of our educational system. As for me, what I perceive moves me to talk more and more.

The crisis in education is not a crisis of the students, it is the manifestation of an ancient and barely visible evil, and it has a positive side, since it is good that the evil become present now. It's like an earache that makes us aware that we should see a doctor. Even though we have spent a long time perpetuating obsolete education, it will no longer be accepted by force by the next generation, and that is good. Remember

---

[1] The idea that the main function of the educational system is to reproduce the social system was formulated by Pierre Bourdieu and others decades ago.

what is said frequently now: how the word "crisis" in the Chinese book of oracles (the *I-Ching* has a hexagram that has this name) is formed by two overlapping ideograms that mean "danger" and "opportunity," respectively. Such is the nature of a crisis. It is not only something bad, but a situation in which there is the potential for discovering that change is needed.

Naturally, the crisis in education is not an isolated event, but an aspect of the functioning of a society in which practically all institutions are in crisis. I have already reiterated what I wrote some ten years ago in "The Agony of the Patriarchy" about how our crisis is not only the crisis of capitalism, of the industrial mentality (as William Harman proposed years before) or an issue of exploitation as Marx proposed.

The crisis, then, is resulting in the breakdown of something much older—an old system that was functional for some time but that has become dangerously obsolete. We can call it the patriarchal system or the patriarchal authority system—a system that is eminently hierarchic—in contrast to what could be a heterarchic system like the ones some companies are beginning to explore by distributing authority in such a way as to have different departments exercise authority with respect to different issues in a more horizontal network.

My work has always been inspired by this vision, that came to me when I was a young man, both through a wise Chilean man who had achieved the "balance of the three" in himself, and through Gurdjieff, who spoke of the lack of integration among our three brains, and today I cannot stop feeling that it is convenient to keep in mind that our problematic educational system is primarily patriarchal, which not only implies that it is at the service of implicit authoritarianism—which perverts our democratic intentions—but that it holds the tyranny of the rational over the affective and the instinctive.

The wish to harmonize and balance the intellectual, emotional and instinctive parts of our nature is widely accepted today, and perhaps that is what we actually mean when we talk about holistic programs. The idea of integrating the Freudian psychic instances, on the other hand, is not less relevant to the ideal of transforming our inner tyranny into a trifocal heterarchy, today supported by therapies derived from psychoanalysis like, for example and most notably, transactional analysis, in spite of the difference in the nomenclature of father, child and adult. Even though the notion of an internal balance of sub-personalities, related to the father, the mother and the child, is familiar to many psychotherapists that observe the healing process, not only has it received little attention up to now, but it has not been proposed as the purpose that is explicit in education or in therapy. I do think it is, however, a fertile idea.

I was saying that patriarchal education, which is the kind we have always known, is a predominantly intellectual education in which all other aspects of the person are underestimated. This is clearly the case of the inner maternal function, that has to do with the limbic brain, linked to love, that we share with our mammal ancestors. We can never stress enough that this aspect suffers from an extreme lack of attention, since today we know that the way in which medicine has disposed our entrance into the world, beginning by birth itself (unnecessarily traumatic in an as yet unknown degree) and continuing into the lactating phase (during which the establishing of the natural link between mother and child is not sufficiently respected) causes damage to the sub-cortical system. The traditional and established form of raising children is already infused with great insensitivity, and school only reinforces setting off the affective or interpersonal aspects of life, the education of the loving capacity that is the basis for good human relations and participation in the community—and that is critically lacking in this world.

At this moment the Dalai Lama is traveling around the world sharing very moving words—words that are simple but also deeply experienced, deeply set in personal wisdom —that we must be kinder, that we must be better people. He says this with such integrity, such conviction and such clarity, that this very simple idea that is not even very original is having great impact. And this is a great thing, because it seems that we attend to so many complicated things that we cannot attend to something so simple. But being able to survive the current world crisis depends greatly on achieving a greater dose of benevolence, a more appreciable level of compassion and simple kindness. Without this kindness, all the technical information possible will not take us far.

Since recovering our loving quality has a lot to do with psychotherapy, we need emotional re-education and therefore something that education currently rejects: educators want nothing to do with therapy, and this is something I will talk about later. But before that I want to point out that education also needs to return to the deeper dimension of mankind. This deep dimension is the spiritual side that education originally attended to: the first schools of our culture (meaning western Christian civilization) came into existence in the Middle Ages in areas where there were churches and the first universities in areas where there were cathedrals. Schools were oriented toward influencing an individual to be a better person, which was, in ancient Christianity, equivalent to being a better Christian. Being a better person then was being a person who followed the path of love and sought to serve the will of God while combating egotistical excesses. With the passing of time, religion was transformed more and more into something contaminated by the world, into a system of patriarchal power, just like all other institutions. And when the renaissance came along, and people were quite tired of the excesses of Christianity, a hunger for knowledge and a desire to recover the connection with the spirit of the Greco-roman culture that had been eclipsed for centuries re-appeared. And so Humanism was born and became a great inspiration for many. There were people like Erasmus, and before him Picco de la Mirandola, Marisilio Ficcino and others within the great Florentine culture that inspired the re-discovery of antiquity, when the classics were studied again with the desire to understand the wisdom of the old philosophers and literates; understanding so many things that the ancient ones had known and that had been forgotten or set aside by a culture that was too austere in its desire to retreat from the world.

A rich education was born in which the heritages of two civilizations (the Judeo-Christian and the Greco-roman) were integrated to become our inheritance. But this education also weakened and became inert and repetitive, a luxury, a decoration, something used for cultural prestige, as in the typical education of a gentleman, all for vanity at the end of the day. And so, little by little, people began to be more interested in reading Latin and Greek than in being able to absorb the wisdom of the ancient ones.

Education was transformed again when the French Revolution came about, at a time that coincided with the apogee of science in culture. Experimental science had been in an incubation period since Bacon and those that rose to power with the French Revolution. At that time there was a great capacity to do things radically differently and people that had no experience in teaching, but knew a lot about chemistry, paleontology, and biology were called into schools. They called people from the Cruvier school, from the Laplace school, etc. As sciences entered the curriculum, humanities lost importance. It was necessary to an extent, since we have two brains, left and right with predominantly analytical and synthetic functions respectively. We can see how it would be desirable to have a balance between science and humanities. But, in agreement with the cultural spirit of the time (the technological world with its faith placed on scientific progress and the implicit equation that says that scientific progress is equal to a good future for the world) emphasis was displaced toward science and that is what banks and governments ask for when financing improvements.

Later in the history of education comes the moment in which there is a separation between Church and State: a great liberation in view of the limiting factor of ecclesiastical power at that time, but also an acute loss described in an English phrase that speaks of "throwing out the baby with the bath water". This is something that happened in education: the idea of spirituality had been so linked through the centuries with the idea of spirituality proper to the Christian church, that no other spiritual education could be conceived other than the old-fashioned religion classes.

But this idea is not true. A vast spiritual inheritance proceeding from all times and places is at our disposition, and on one occasion I heard Bishop Myers—who I was closely acquainted with—say, "We cannot allow ourselves less than to become true heirs to the complete cultural treasure of humanity." I was surprised to hear him say that since I had never heard a Christian leader say something akin to saying that it was no longer justifiable to ignore the thoughts of Buddha, Lao-Tse, or Mahomet because of living within a limiting sectarianism. We must aspire to a universal culture that considers the messages of great geniuses, the founders of religions, the great messengers, the inspired and the prophets of all cultures, since they have been the ones who have taught us the most, and a sensible education has to do much more than inform us about wars and combats. More than patriotic exaltation, we need an understanding of cultural history and especially of universal spiritual culture. And not only this, but a culture supported by experience: a culture in which there can be workshops in which young people can experience basic spiritual exercises like the forms of meditation characteristic to different cultures. In that way, the person that goes through an educational establishment would have the sense that something touched him, that he would like to investigate more into something special, that something may help him in his ulterior development. In that way, when he goes out into life, he could find more. Just as in places where wine is made there is the opportunity to try wines from different harvests, why not in education? This could offer the different flavors of religious experience from different spiritual practices.

Up to now this has not been done because the taboo against spirituality has not allowed it: it has not been allowed to re-import spirituality in a creative and novel way.

And something similar, in my opinion, has happened in the therapeutic world.

Currently in schools there is a taboo toward the therapeutic world, a taboo that sometimes takes on the form of "not wanting complications"; "what happens if the students start to talk about what happens at home and the parents come to complain," "surely the parents won't like it if students share things that happen at home in school," and all other sorts of excuses; but it weighs on teachers not to be able to face the Pandora's box that could open and the fear that the potential chaos that could come from facing these truths would interrupt their task of teaching.

I believe that the historic antecedent of this conflict is the interest that educators had in learning about psychoanalysis when it made its entrance into the world with the pretense of having discovered the great truths of the psychic world. But today we know that psychoanalysis fell short of its pretensions, that it was a very dogmatic formulation, and that we can retrospectively see that the world, naively, accepted this dogmatism and then was disappointed. There were radical experiences, like those of Summerhill, O'Neal (enthusiastic Reichian who took permissiveness to levels that were not well-known). But only permissiveness and Freudian ideas would not take us far. Education is much more complex and I believe educators showed good sense in putting distance between themselves and a possible invasion by psychoanalytic authorities. Psychoanalysis is a very authoritarian system, like a church that moves based on faith. This becomes plainly visible only now when this school, that was a monolithic block, has been divided into many, and the degree of discrepancy between the branches or varieties of psychoanalysis is such that we can no longer say that any of the characteristic fundamental ideas (like the death drive or the Oedipal complex) has survived in terms of generalized acceptance.

There were other attempts to bring psychotherapy into schools in the 60's and I was a witness to this in the United States because I was part of that humanistic movement. There were enthusiasts that organized Rogerian encounter groups or "sensitivity training" in schools, but the results were not very convincing. More problems opened up than could be dealt with and closed, and some people were very interested while others were hurt or behaved antagonistically.

I would say that these attempts to bring psychology prematurely into schools caused disappointment, mistrust and rejection of any new attempts. Now we have better means and resources, but they still haven't made their way to educators, not even to universities. They generally arrive late and there are things that are more frequently discovered outside of the university than inside. One of my professors, Eduardo Cruz Coke, an inspired man who taught biochemistry in medical school and who was also a Chilean politician, used to say, "When we find a cure for cancer it will surely not be in one of the hundreds of institutions that are dedicated to cancer research. It will be discovered outside, in the cracks in the institutional." There is much truth to that, and in psychology it has been confirmed that the academic world is the last to know about contributions to human development that are truly worthwhile. And the reason is that the academic world suffers from the perversions of the patriarchal world. Reading Freud lately—for me who once was a fervent Freudian, since my first formation was psychoanalytical before going on to Gestalt and other things—causes in me a combination of admiration and embarrassment because in his theoretical mania there is a great disconnection from the obvious.

The patriarchal scientificism of our academic environment reminds me of the famous joke about the German man who had a systematic and extremely fast way to learn languages. With his heavy German accent, he explained it all to his friend: "In the first place, one day for the verb; then one day for the noun; the third day for the adjective, and the fourth day for the prepositions, conjunctions and interjections. And at the end a few days dedicated exclusively to vocabulary: lots and lots of vocabulary in order to get it all into"—and pointing at his own head—"your ass."

The unconscious dogmatism that makes us laugh at this personification of rigid intellectualism is not essentially different from what today has contaminated official psychology: it speaks—as did Freud, in spite of his noble heritage—with the certainty of one who feels he is the owner of the truth, a certainty which in turn allows him to proclaim fundamental errors.

I believe, therefore, that education needs to get over these two taboos: the taboo against everything therapeutic and the taboo against everything spiritual. And those would be obstacles enough. But even if those taboos are overcome, there is another obstacle yet: when someone presents the ideal of holistic education to someone who works in the educational bureaucracy the answer is, in not so many words perhaps: "But where are we going to get money for such a fundamental reform?"

If we are to have education oriented toward human development, we must pass over the monopoly of the intellectual to a very economical pedagogy as far as theory is concerned: an education that carefully avoids redundancy and that supports itself with computers and audiovisual material in order not to waste teachers on the nearly mechanical function they have today. Teachers would have to return to the human function of interpersonal re-education and help in community development (functions that are barely touched on by the current notion of education in values, in spite of the good intentions that this type of program holds). And the proposal that we move toward an education that is truly more relevant for life would have to give first importance to self-knowledge, which means, together with wishing to apply education to happy interpersonal relations, a re-education for educators. We cannot deceive ourselves: self-knowledge is something we bow to only on the surface. Since we consider ourselves heirs to the Oracle of Delphos, to Socrates, and to the rest of the ancient philosophers, we all agree that the exclusive attention paid to knowledge of the world at the dawn of philosophy was overcome when man, capable of self-reflection, began to be interested in himself. But, how can we take into account this high ideal of self-knowledge within the education that is offered today? Not even offering a branch called "psychology" do we really involve a discipline of self-knowledge, but instead an exposition of various behaviorist theories, dynamic psychology, constructivism, and other schools; but never a living psychology that helps students to face their own reality.

And nevertheless it is possible to incorporate self-knowledge into the curriculum; and in answer to the objection that says that complementing the current training for professionals would be too expensive, I can answer—and this is the most important thing that I can say—that I know that is not true. I well know that it can be done economically, because I have proven over and over that what is lacking now in training programs for teachers can be added in the form of a supplementary curriculum that includes self-knowledge, interpersonal re-education and spiritual culture that takes no more than 10 days per year in three successive modules.

How can I be so sure? Not because I've done the experiment with a homogenous group of educators, but because I've done something very similar with psychotherapists. And I've developed a way to teach psychotherapists—in training or already out of college —to be of more efficient service, through a teaching that is not only technical but that is also based on relevant personal experience —beginning with self-understanding—that is an indispensable basis for understanding others and also for developing a benevolent interest in others.

Many educators have come to my courses, and they all leave feeling that this is what education needs: a universalist non-dogmatic spiritual injection that includes concrete practices that serve to cultivate the deepest mind—beginning by cultivating attention—and a guided process of self-knowledge that not only allows changes in conduct, but allows a much deeper transformation that is the essence of human maturity.

Perhaps some have asked themselves what the secret is, and I'll explain it briefly: the fact that there can be a deep transforming and humanizing impact in such brief interventions is due in part to the existence of resources that were unknown or not taken advantage of before (like the psychology of the Enneatypes or meditation or Gestalt therapy); also to new resources (like certain types of therapeutic acting that is based on the psychology of the Enneatypes or on our integrative psychotherapy laboratory); and to the organization of these resources into a whole that is greater than the sum of its parts. This has been, also, to an extent, the result of the evolution of a living process and a growing experience put together by me and the people who have collaborated with me as teachers.

It would be too much here to describe the mosaic that makes up the self-knowledge and interpersonal re-education program that I have been using for some 12 years in the form of intensive encounters in three modules over consecutive years. Suffice it to say that it has been described as a process of humanization and opening to love, and that, from another point of view it could well be described as a "mill for grinding egos" since it took inspiration from the vision of a spiritual path as an awakening, through the consciousness of the ego to the consciousness of being, and it is implemented through a guided group process that leads to insights (interpersonal and intrapersonal), confrontation of the individual personality, cultivation of neutrality and voluntary inhibition of neurotic needs (the sins and obstacles of traditional paths).

The theoretical part that is a complement to the combination of meditative and therapeutic work within the program includes, among other aspects, the application of the Enneagram of the personality—an inheritance left by Oscar Ichazo that I have refined over the past 30 years and that becomes strongly present in the minds of participants as a map of the work applied to diverse circumstances—and that includes a series of elements such as interpersonal therapeutic exercises, drama, community life and psycho-corporal work.

The fundamental influence throughout the evolution of my activity has come from Gurdieff, who emphasized working on all levels or centers: action, emotion, and intellect—as well as the cultivation of attention: being present in the here and now. It was natural, then, to use the movements created by Gurdieff for the motor aspect of the work. I stopped using them, however, a short time after I arrived in California from Taiwan and having worked with the Taoist master Ch'u Fang Chu, wanting to take advantage of his high level of competence in Tai Chi and associated practices. After his death I have had the collaboration of Gerda Alexander (from Eutony), of Graciela Figueroa (dancer and instructor in Río Abierto) and others.

The most relevant point is, however, that just as electronic devices have become smaller and more efficient over the years, this program, that at the beginning lasted three months (over three years), has been reduced to three annual meetings of ten days, each preceded by an introductory program of five days—with the results becoming more owerful, so much so that in Spain there are comments that the SAT program has had a favorable impact on the professional competency of the country.

In Spain, and in Brazil, the educational law has introduced the concept of "transversalities" in reference to an ethical education oriented toward universal values. The hope is that teachers can facilitate the concept in the way that they put the traditional curriculum into practice.

Magnificent idea, truly—that hints at the intuition that says that education takes place through spontaneous contagion, from person to person, of wisdom and love. In practice, however, only someone who lives these values can take advantage of the opportunities to share them; and in order to do this the combination of instruction and sermonizing that is called "an education in values" is not enough.

In order to effectively be more generous and supportive, for example, it is not enough to hold the conviction that solidarity or generosity are important, and so, simple exhortation does not go far. Added to that is the limited inspiration that they can be transmitted through reasons or beautiful words. Just as life only comes from life, consciousness can only be woken by consciousness. We need, therefore, a third element from among the branches of classical curriculum and the education in values that we have wished to reach through transversalities: the transformation of the educator—for which the educators themselves need to go through a process of un-identification with childhood conditionings (the "ego") and of liberation of their essential beings.

The most important thing I can contribute, at the moment, is the news that this can be done relatively briefly and economically—and I say this after a dozen years in which I've seen that the majority of the people who go through our workshops not only come out with a greater capacity to help others, but feeling themselves living on a different level of life.

At seventy years of age I am naturally on my way to retirement, and I have begun to delegate my work to my disciples. For years I have felt reiterated satisfaction of being able to effectively help many and of being bathed in their gratitude, and just when I feel that the SAT program, refined year after year, is now fruit ready to be picked, it seems as though it may fall from the tree it grew on onto soil that is different from its origin.

I am pleased to think that the deep experience of transformation that has served therapists in a better functioning in their work, can someday serve educators as well, and through them serve to overcome or transform the limitations of an implicitly oppressive system that, perpetuating our fundamental ignorance, marches against our attempts to establish healthy relationships.

## 5. Educating the Whole Person in Order to Build a Unified World

*"Almost all education is motivated by politics: in order to strengthen a social, religious or national group in competition with other groups. This is the main motivation that determines what subjects will be taught, what knowledge will be offered, and what knowledge will be hidden, and that will also determine the mental habits that students will be expected to cultivate. Practically nothing is done taking into account the inner development of the mind and the spirit; in effect, those who have received higher levels of education have often suffered from mental and spiritual atrophy."*

Bertrand Russell, in Grace Llewelyn, Op. cit.

*"A little knowledge of superior things is more valuable than a lot of knowledge of inferior things."*

Thomas Aquinas

$\mathbf{A}$ lot is said today about a "change in paradigms" in science and, more generally, in the way we understand the world and humankind. What is this new paradigm, invoked by new physics and contemporary psychology and that, more or less implicitly, is affecting almost all fields of knowing and doing?

We could call it "holism" or "integralism": a focus centered on the whole. This is the perspective that underlies inspirations as diverse as the general theory of systems, the systemic focus in administrative sciences and business management, structuralism, and the psychology of form. The most outstanding characteristic of our era is a new way to conceive structures, organizations, and the interrelationship of the parts of a whole. Life and the universe show themselves to us today as evolutionary meta-structures.

Some 2,500 years ago Buddha told the story of some blind men who each formed an idea of what an elephant was like in relation to the part of the elephant that each of them touched, comparing it to a palm tree, a rope, a fan, etc., according to whether the hands of the person were touching a leg, the tail, an ear, or other parts of the animal. This story, picked up later by the Sufis, has become particularly popular today, and rightly so, since it expresses the blossoming of the spirit in our time of ever more generalized understanding, that the whole is, quite effectively, more than the sum of its parts.

This change in our perspective of the world is without a doubt a reflection of a living process: if in the intellectual area we are in an era of holism, in more general terms we could say that we are in an era of synthesis. Not only have we become more interdisciplinary, more ecumenical, more intercultural, but we are feeling more and more the need to become complete people in a unified world.

Holistic education, along with the holistic focus of reality in general, is part of this synthesizing tendency that is afoot. It was Rousseau, the father of romanticism and the grandfather of the French revolution, who first brought attention to the capital importance of educating feelings. Then others, like Dewey, Maria Montessori and Piaget, put the accent on learning through doing. On the other hand, Steiner and the Waldorf Schools that are based on his work, insist in developing intuition and in what we now call transpersonal education. More recently, the Human Potential Movement has induced experimentation of the "affective area" in education. Holistic Education proposes uniting all these dispersed voices, in a project that would take on the entire person: body, emotions, intellect and spirit.

Besides being called holistic because of the pretense of educating the complete person, I think that education should be holistic in other aspects as well: for example, in striving for an integration of knowledge, in its interest in intercultural integration, in its planetary vision of things, in its balance between theory and practice, in paying attention to the future as well as to the past and present. A particularly critical issue should be, naturally, the balance between the "paternal", "maternal" and "filial" aspects of the person. For that reason I'm inclined to talk about "integral education" in reference to the educational holism that is coming to be and that I personally support.

While in the USA things have evolved from the "revolution of the conscious" to growing conservativeness in the 80's, the idea of integrative and comprehensive education has bumped into the question of whether it is a luxury or not. Without making reference to any specific type of education, for example, Yankelevich writes in one of his recently published books, *New Rules*, that the world situation is becoming so critical and the situation for individuals is becoming so difficult, that there is no more time to search for "self-realization". The days of the Human Potential Movement, according to him, should be considered things of the past, as a reflection of the transitory situation of abundance that was prevalent when it came about.

I think we should be careful with this type of opinion that is nothing more than a regression to the excessively practical and "realistic" attitude that is the origin of the current problematic situation. It is precisely the urgency of the problems that we are faced with as a species today that make it imperative, and not a luxury, to set out on the educational task with a new focus. As Botkin and others say in their report to the Club of Rome, *No Limits to Learning*[1]:

"After a decade of talking about general topics, some signs of change have been seen in the debates. The majority of the participants in extensive conferences centered on proposing new models of construction for the world have felt that the dialogs were lacking an elemental critical sense. The concern for the material aspect of world problems have effectively taken over the propositions. It has now become evident that there is a new concern: putting human beings

---

[1] *No Limits to Learning: Bridging the Human Gap*, James W. Botkin, Mahdi Elmandjara and Mircea Maletza, Pergamon Press, 1979.

back in the center of the problematic situation. This presupposes a change, in the sense of no longer considering global problems as manifestations of physical problems of material survival (Life Support System), in order to begin to accept the preeminent importance of the human aspect of said problems." These writers talk about the "Human Gap" that mankind is now faced with—the distance between the growing complexity of problems and man's capacity to deal with them—and they think this gap can be overcome by using learning as a bridge:

"Learning, in this sense, goes much further that one more general topic. Failure in this area is currently, in a fundamental way, the central topic of world problems. In summary, learning has become an issue of life or death."

I personally prefer to emphasize "development" and to say that if we continue living as caterpillars, refusing to become butterflies, we will destroy our environment and devour each other. To put it in other words, we cannot allow ourselves to continue to set aside, even as just a possibility, the transformation of mankind that has taken place in all eras. What in other times was just the destiny of a few, and could have been seen as a luxury, now has the characteristic of collective urgency. Today the growth of power that mankind has available amplifies the effects of the abuses committed in its use, and the consequences are inevitable for a population that is threatening to surpass the capacity limits of the planet. And in it all we cannot help but see the expression of a psyche that is only very incompletely developed.

The psychology of ordinary human beings— psychology that we would have to call "normal"—is, psychoanalytically speaking, regressive. Under the guise of pseudo-abundance that we flaunt before the world, and with which we identify, our motivation comes generally from what we don't have: we are greedy, we feel unsatisfied and dependent. In other times, in the times of our Cro-Magnon ancestors, we were cannibals, but judging by the way international affairs go we are implicitly cannibals still. Military expenditures in the world in 1979 exceeded one billion dollars a day, and in later years, during which scarcity and overpopulation have become threatening, they only increased more. Would this be necessary if we were not, on an unconscious level, a paranoid and cannibalistic society? Would it not be reasonable to allot that sum of money to an Earth restoration program that could include as most urgent the needs for ecological attention and the development of consciousness?

Our collective life, in the very dawn of prehistory, faced challenges that stimulated our ancestors to evolve, but also traumas that drew us into an abyss of psychosocial pathology. The motivation that comes from what is lacking— and the resulting exploitation of others has been perpetuated by contagion, infecting generation after generation with the psychic condition of the humans that have gone before us, so that currently we are pushed toward eminent shipwreck from which we can only save ourselves if we know how to swim, and I use the metaphor "swim" to name the new consciousness capable of taking us from "here" to "there", from the obsolete conditioning we are suffering from to a new world order.

Far from being a luxury, a new education—an education of the whole person for the entire world—is an urgent need, and it is also our greatest hope: all of our problems would be greatly simplified just by reaching true mental health, since this would lead to an authentic capacity to love. As Krishnamurti said years ago, "Individual peace is the foundation on which world peace sits."

Today the majority of the people that were part of a generation of seekers, perhaps only comparable to those who existed in the times of the first Christians or the forming of other great religions, are still alive. This cultural phenomenon, which exploded in the United States some 30 years ago, has gone through a period of enthusiastic expansion and another of disappointed waning, and that reflects the structure of a psychological process. After all that well-known enthusiasm when beginning the journey, when it seemed that the whole world would soon be transformed, a considerable fraction of that North American youth had advanced toward the equally well-known stage of realizing that—as Gurdjieff used to say—"at the beginning there are roses, roses, roses; then thorns, thorns, thorns." Every generation, practically speaking, has set out on that search; however, up to now we have not seen a transformed society as a result, but only a handful of wizards' apprentices in different degrees of development:   individuals only partially transformed, that have something to give from their experience and now know that the journey is much harder and longer than they thought.

If it is so difficult to transform an adult, it may be easier to begin with young people.  If we think in terms of a global perspective, taking into account the most vital needs that incite us as inhabitants of this Earth, education, and in particular all the help we can get in growing as human beings during the stages of greater plasticity, would shine above all other possible strategies as the most adequate in order to be able to intervene consciously in our own evolutionary transformation.  Certainly, it is also the most economic, in a time when the economic factor is crucial.

Hitler discovered in his time that by controlling education he could control society.  We could rescue the truth hidden in that perception, and place it on a true foundation, since it is not through "control" that we will reach the objective we desire, but through habits of attention, ability and affection, and more than anything else through the quality of being.  Only by giving young people the possibility to become complete human beings can we expect a better world.  If we are to "control" education, we need to understand that this control must be but at the service of the liberation of individuals—in reality it would be better to call it counter-control.

This slogan is familiar to many of us: "Form men that the country needs."  If we attend to the implicit meaning of this expression, formation here is a synonym for socialization in general terms, in other words, education conceived as a vehicle for social conditioning.  But if we speak about forming men the world needs, we must then admit that we would not as a necessity educate from and for conformism, but for freedom and autonomy, since a "true" world would only be possible if we have authentic individuals.

Writing after Darwin did, Herbert Spencer compared society to an organism—an idea that later sociologists left out. Truly, our society is far from being an organism, and in that we have advanced less than bees and ants. A society that is, with respect to the individual, what the brain is to the cells that make it up, would have to be based on the existence of mature human beings, in other words, integrated beings that are on the road to self-realization, and not the species of humanoid robots that our society promotes in its blindness and other maladies.

It could be said that an education oriented toward the entire person is in itself oriented toward a totality that is even vaster, that it would be an "education for a unified world", and I have wished to emphasize this idea by including it as the title of this chapter. In the first place, it is to underline the thesis that "education of the whole person is education for the whole world", and also because of how healthy it would be to specifically accentuate the meta-personal objective. Besides, it is an inspiring idea: if we become conscious of how greatly education oriented toward peace and world unity is needed, perhaps this consciousness may cause the corresponding creative capacity that the objective requires.

An individual cannot truly consider himself complete if he doesn't have a global vision of the world, if he has no sense of brotherhood. We need a form of education that takes the individual to this point of maturity in which, rising above the isolated perspective of the "I" and of tribal mentality he reaches a fully developed communitarian sense and a planetary perspective. We need a form of education for the individual as part of humanity, an education in the feeling of humanity.

The spiritual awakening that forms part of our potential destiny does not take into account only the birth of the "I" but also the birth of the "you." The birth of the being takes into account the birth of the "I-you," the birth of the sense of "us."

How can education contribute to the creation of the sense of "us"? Not only through an attitude that strays from localism and is open to a universal vision of things, but, first and foremost, through an expert application of techniques of community leadership, meaning with tried and true help in group forming processes in the true sense of the expression.

For Carl Rogers groups were possibly the most significant invention of this century. The future will tell. But in any case they are an important resource, and I believe all educators should acquire a repertoire of abilities that include, among other things, the capacity to facilitate sincere communication among students—while being responsible for the consequences—the capacity to recognize and express individual perceptions, one's own and those of others, and to develop empathy and stay clear of the games the ego plays. This process should not, however, be limited to the celebration of group encounters and other events, but make up the background of all educational situations. There are two kinds of groups that, because they represent other powerful forms of communitarian activity, I would like to stress. One is the task group that offers an ideal situation for learning collaborative work as well as for developing the consciousness of the problems that make it difficult. The other is the decision making group that, besides offering the participants a clear reflection of their character, makes up, perhaps, the most fundamental instrument we have in function of education for democracy.

When we apply all these resources, we should keep in mind that, in our current situation, growth and healing are inseparable. Only artificially can the field of education be separated from the field of psychotherapy and the spiritual disciplines, since there is only one unique process of growth-healing-enlightenment. The taboo that opposes the introduction of psychotherapy in education should be considered a regressive and defensive symptom, which it truly is. If we continue to ignore the affective field in education, we will continue to give back to the world individuals who are fixated in childhood behavior, feelings and thought patterns, and surely we will be getting ever further from the objective of educating people to develop in plenitude.

After having invested so many words it is time to put into practice the idea of integral education. I would like to point out, be it only partially, what my vision is of what education could be like in the future. And to start off I cannot avoid remembering the essay that Aldous Huxley wrote on the topic: "On the Education of an Amphibian." The observations and suggestions that follow are nothing more than an update on the pioneering invitation that Huxley launched in favor of holistic education more than thirty years ago.

"It is not necessary to repeat that the new form of education is to be aimed at the body, the emotions, the mind and the spirit; but how and with what tools?

With respect to physical education, we know enough today to see that besides training in sports and other means of maintaining adequate physical condition, there are other more subtle means of body working. It is the field that Dr. Thomas Hanna named "New Somatology". We could speak of internal and external body work, following the application of these terms in sports. What is new is that it is necessary to add attitude and attention to traditional physical education, and also it would be wise to add to the curriculum some form of sensory-motor training. Not only would some working techniques based on movement, like Self-consciousness through Movement used in Feldenkreis, Eutony by Gerda Alexander, or relational psycho-motor education, be excellent and appropriate, but also some traditional focuses like Hatha Yoga and Tai-Chi-Chuan.

Another field, related also to the physical aspect of the human Holon, and needing attention, is the field that has to do with what we could call skills, whether it be in the area of domestic care, culinary arts or general artisan work. If the psychopathological side interferes with the capability of movement in order to perform any task, it is clear that the cultivation of a healthy attitude with respect to one's own activity has indubitable therapeutic value. Manual work offers valuable opportunities to develop deep-set virtues such as patience and the capacity for self-satisfaction, only by knowing how to appreciate the inner value hidden in any art form and learning to use an external situation for one's own growth as a person.

Let us look now at emotional education. In the first place, we have to say that it would be artificial to separate affective education too much from the area of education in interpersonal relations, and equally, we cannot separate the affective interpersonal field from the topic of self-knowledge. As to this, I wish to point out that everything included in the area of interpersonal education, whether it is self-knowledge, self-study, or self-understanding—that high ideal so ardently assumed and preached by Socrates—is something that current educational models systematically set aside in times during which we have enough resources to do something different. It is time to have modernly conceived human communications laboratories in our programs where the ability for self-understanding is promoted and facilitated in a context of interpersonal awareness and communicative learning, based on the many resources available today, from the free association exercises that Freud introduced, to the latest refinings of the humanistic movement.

Of course, we need to develop, if not recover, the capacity to identify our own feelings, as well as to express them authentically and adequately. We cannot allow ourselves to skip over the contribution made by dramatization techniques, and more generally, expression techniques, for the development of emotional life. A resource that comes from the liberal conception of education is also important here: contact with the literary and artistic patrimony of the entire world, under adequate guidance. This is an inheritance passed from heart to heart, just as science and philosophy are inheritances passed from mind to mind.

The most important thing I have to say, however, with respect to education in the affective field, would be the need we have to recognize that the main objective is the development of the capacity to love.

There is no doubt that health and all of its natural concomitant virtues are inseparable from the ability to love oneself and to love others. So, we need a teaching of love. We have enough information to develop it; perhaps what was missing was a sense of direction and the occasion to apply it in an educational environment. We know, for example, that besides the need for warmth, understanding and psychological security, and also providing the occasion for developing the feeling of community, it is necessary to deal adequately with childhood ambivalence in which the great majority of our society grows up as a result of having parents who are everything but emotionally mature, happy and productive beings. The loving potential of an individual is veiled by his hate for himself and by his destructiveness, whether it is conscious or unconscious; all things that were developed in his earliest history. Freeing ourselves from this, as shown currently by the psychotherapeutic experience, demands a high degree of intuitive rather than purely intellectual understanding in the re-examination of life and the ventilation of all the pain and frustration associated with past impressions in order to let them go. Of course, this all normally requires a long psychotherapeutic process, but even so, today it can be done much faster than in the times when psychoanalytical exploration reigned.

I believe that all of this is due in a large part to the taboo that exists in the educational field with respect to the therapeutic field, as well as with respect to the topic of religion. It is expected that the educational field should be separate and not be invaded by these other fields. This is a somewhat territorial conception, exacerbated in reality by understandable complications, like what happens when a child begins to talk in school about what happens at home. These are not things that can be handled on a local level in the school itself. The teachers, the administrators, even educational bureaucrats need to have stronger support in order to take the initiative to set up elements in schools that form part of the methodology—we could say of the technology—that we have today for the development of and/or healing of affective relationships. If the crisis we are going through is above all a crisis of relations, a crisis in relation to the loving capacity of mankind, we cannot continue to maintain the separation between the therapeutic area and the educational area, nor can we continue to identify education with often irrelevant instruction.

Perhaps the resource from the field of humanistic psychology that has been applied in education most, at least in the USA, has been the Gestalt focus (taking on the name "confluent education"). George Brown, professor of education at the Santa Barbara campus of the University of California, and a Gestalt therapist, received support from the Esalen Institute and the Ford Foundation more than 20 years ago, and has been giving Gestalt formation to educators systematically for all these years, not so much so that Gestalt therapy would become an additional part of the program, but in order to give the teachers a better understanding of the human condition, and a greater ability to handle themselves as human beings when with other human beings —all which means work in the border area between didactics and therapy. I believe that Gestalt deserves to be recommended as a first level resource because it is so economical: a brief contact with Gestalt can raise a person's level in these abilities, by returning to the person the option of being in the here and now. Most people live under an implicit taboo that does not allow them to express what is happening at the moment, so when they acquire the capacity to be more conscious and assume the responsibility of their experience in the here and now, thousands of new things can appear. This is a liberation that is loaded with consequences. When someone can interrupt what is happening on a discursive level to say, for example, "Something smells bad," or, "I'm uncomfortable," or, "This situation bores me," they move communication to the interpersonal level, and it becomes possible to overcome many sterile stagnant experiences.

Something similar could be said for Transactional Analysis, psychodrama, and diverse other contemporary therapies. They deserve to be part of the ideal mosaic of experience and would contribute as much to the process of personal development as the professional formation of educators. But, while dreaming of possible future education, I want to emphasize the enormous potential that is found in a therapeutic focus not very well known yet, even among therapists, and that is known as the Fischer-Hoffman Process. It did not originate in the academic world, but in the spiritual world, and I give it singular relevance as a remedy for patriarchal evils, since it is a method that is specifically oriented toward integrating the inner "father," "mother," and "child." It is also known as the "Quadrinity Process" in that it seeks to harmonize body, emotions, intellect, and spirit in the individual. More than 10 years ago, in one of the international Gestalt congresses held in the United States, I recommended this process as very appropriate for forming Gestalt therapists and in general as recommended in the formation of any type of therapist. But I think the main potential of this method is in education. It manages, relatively easily, to plant a healing seed in a short time in the area that is the specialty of this method: the relationships the person has with his parents, whether they are still alive or not. The idea is the same as the fourth commandment, since lack of love or the ambivalence toward parents and conscious or repressed aggression toward them perturbs the relationships that the person has with the entire world, and that is (using psychoanalytical terms) what is behind the "repetition compulsion", interminably transferring to the present the attitudes learned in the past. If the loving link is reestablished with the parents (a loving link that the majority don't even suspect they have lost), the possibility is reopened for a different level of love toward themselves, and as a result toward others.

If we wished to establish which aspect within the area of educating the intellect is more in need of reform, it would be necessary to point out something very different from what is gone over and proposed year after year in innumerable educational congresses on a national and global level and which receive large sums of money. In the United States and in other countries millions of dollars are invested in educational reform that does no more than reform the curriculum, most of the time just by slightly varying the same topics. What is necessary is not so much to modify as to significantly condense the traditional curriculum based on a serious process of selection that has barely begun and implement what I would call an ethics of economy in the area of resources and the area of the use of the students' time in such a way as to make the school situation an experience in favor of the child, one that would bear fruit from a perspective that pays more attention to human values.

We could expect that with respect to the cognitive area of education there would be less to say or do in favor of possible improvement, since up to now education has almost exclusively concentrated on this aspect. However, education in its intellectual aspect needs to go much further than just transmitting information, whether the objective is to understand the world better or to make the individual able to perform specific tasks in the world.

Extending education beyond cognitive content, as I am suggesting, brings us face to face with the need to develop the informative angle in schools in a much more efficient way than it has been up to now, simply because there would be much less time to spend on it. We need to take maximum advantage of all the potential that puzzles and games hold, as an ideal means to include early learning in mathematics, deploy all the richness of audiovisual resources, explore the possibilities of computers, etc. And I believe, above all, that we need what could be called an ethics of briefness: we can no longer allow ourselves to overload the storage capacity of our brains with detailed information on non-essential things or aspects, but we must concentrate completely on really significant issues, whether they are in relation to our vision of the world or our preparation to be of service to the world. The hunger for understanding is part of human nature and it needs to be fed from a panoramic vision of knowledge. It would be advisable, then, and wise, to set up a type of education that includes a balance between generalization and specialization; meaning an education that is capable of promoting specific abilities backed up by general contents. This in itself would imply educating, in a certain way, what we call integrative thought.

What our current panorama shows as insufficiently emphasized in traditional education is the development of cognitive abilities as such, above and beyond contents to be learned. Besides learning, we need, above all, to learn to learn. Even if we adopt an attitude that is more pragmatic than humanistic, we come to the same conclusion. "The amount of knowledge that one acquires in any area of contents has no relation to, generally speaking, better performance in the corresponding occupation," writes Professor Kilpatrick in the AHHP (Architectural History and Historic Preservation Division) Bulletin, "The majority of occupations only require that the individual is willing and capable. What distinguishes the efficient individual in the performance of his function is not so much the acquisition or the use of knowledge, but the cognitive capabilities developed and exercised in the process of acquiring and using that knowledge". Here we also need to move our focus of attention from the external to the internal, from the apparent to the subtle.

In order to develop cognitive capabilities, there are new resources that education could incorporate today, tools that go from the lateral thought exercises of De Bono and the training in implicit supposition analysis[2], to dialectic thought and the non-verbal education of Feuerstein, among others. I wish to emphasize, however, two resources that, although they are not so new, should not fall into disuse. First of all, I'm referring to mathematics. This is an area with contents that are extraordinarily valuable in educating reasoning as such, as

---

[2]Cf., for example, the book by Abercrombie, *Anatomy of Judgment*, and the book by Mayfield, *Thinking for Yourself.*

educators of the past well knew. If we aspire to balance the left and right hemispheres of the brain, we should be very careful not to throw mathematics overboard as if they were a part of academics that belongs to the past, as the thinking of the new culture centered on the right brain seems inclined to do. In second place, I am referring to music. All creative expression, no matter the means, can be considered a means by which to develop intuition, but among them all music stands out, just as mathematics stands out from all other sciences. Music, as Polanyi said, is "sensitive mathematics" and it can do for our intuitive brain what mathematics does for our rational brain. In this aspect we may be able to learn something from Hungarians who, under the direction of Zoltan Kodali, for about two decades now, have been pioneering the field of musical education and the observation of the benefits it has on the children, showing measurable results in the area of the development of intelligence. There are also other resources available in this area that our schools could benefit from, like the Orff system and Dalcroze's Eurritmia.

Another aspect of an education centered on the loving capacity is transpersonal or spiritual education. Half of what we can do in this respect is made up of promoting the destruction of the "ego," teaching students to transcend their own character and offering help in the process of liberating themselves from inner obstacles. The other half would be centered on cultivating the qualities that are inherent in all forms of meditation, since it is well-known and preached by all religions that love flows naturally in mystical experiences.

This connects with the topic of transpersonal education, in other words, the education of that aspect of the person that is beyond the body, the mind and the emotions, and that traditionally is given the name "spirit." I will begin by mentioning the controversial question as to whether religion should or should not be taught in schools. There was a time when religion was a mandatory subject. Then, secular education claimed its independence from the church, and that was to be a step forward in the development of modern society. But one thing is becoming independent from the authority of a determined religious hierarchy, and another altogether to speak of spiritual education. The religious angle is an aspect of human nature and no education can be called holistic if it doesn't take that into account. The spirit of our times cannot be reconciled with promoting any type of dogma or particular attitudes: the time has come for a trans-systemic and trans-cultural focus in the area of the spirit. As I once heard Bishop Myers of San Francisco say in a prospective[3] meeting: "We can no longer continue to be unfamiliar with the entire spiritual inheritance of humanity." What we need is obviously a "type of religion" that presents the essence of spiritual teachings from the entire world and underlines the common universal experience that they all symbolize, interpret and cultivate in different ways.

I also wish to touch on the question of when a child should be initiated in religious education. There are certain practices that are steeped in the spiritual significance that is in a way equivalent to that found in meditation, and that are appropriate for small children, such as the contact with nature, art, crafts, dance and body work, and above all storytelling and guided fantasy. Nevertheless, in my opinion, the ideal time to begin explicit spiritual education is in puberty and not before, unless we wish to participate in brain washing. Primitive cultures that, as we well know today, can be very much evolved spiritually, introduce their members to symbols and revelations of their tradition during the rite of initiation to adolescence and to adult life. Before that, religious matters are treated as mysteries for which there will be sufficient opportunity and accompaniment when the time comes. I think this much extended practice holds much wisdom, since it is in adolescence when the passion to understand the metaphysical surfaces, making many young people into natural philosophers. And, more important yet, adolescence marks the beginning of dreaming, the waking of energy that moves the seeker to seek. It is, then, the time that is biologically

---

[3]Prospective: a set of analyses and studies done in order to explore or foresee the future.

adequate for the growing individual to know about his "journey" and his objective, and about the help, the vehicles, the tools, and the talismans that he can use.

It is not necessary to say that authentic spiritual education should not remain in the theoretical territory, and that spiritual teachings should offer an adequate context for practice. If the curriculum is to have a "religion class", it should be complemented by a life experience introduction to spiritual disciplines, in a sort of "religion laboratory" that includes introduction to meditation and other similar practices, so that the individual, upon leaving school, has sufficient basic tools for spiritual progress in daily life.

Some time will have to pass before we can ensure individuals that are capable of setting up learning in the area of spiritual disciplines based on experimentation and designed from a trans-cultural and integral perspective. Meanwhile, the best option could be to offer students a period of time during which they can "try" a selection of the main spiritual disciplines cultivated in the world. For this, adequate guides would have to be available. I hope in the future we can have the opportunity to design a trans-systemic program of spiritual practices conceived in accordance with the natural elements and objectives of all spiritual teaching and with the aspects of the psychic process they imply. It is clear, for example, that a natural form of initiating a program like this would be based on the practice of concentration, since all forms of meditation, cult and prayer rest on the capacity for correct concentration.

Although this topic, which is one of my fields of specialization, deserves to be developed much more extensively, I would just like to say here that the existing variety of types of spiritual practice can be reduced, in my opinion, to a series of pure forms, or a combination of a limited number of "internal actions," and I think that just as physical education requires the exercising of different possibilities of movement of the body, so should we also try to cultivate different "psychological postures" that are implied in the spiritual experience; in effect, this optimum attitude of the conscience that all spiritual disciplines pursue as their goal includes multifaceted experiences and a state that has diverse qualities and sensations such as clarity, calm, liberty, detachment, love and sacredness. And although the cultivation of each of these qualities is a path in itself, something could be gained through an integrative focus that, above and beyond what each of them represents, points to the objective at which they all converge.

Besides efficiency, a program conceived based on the comprehension of underlying dimensions in all spiritual practices would have the advantage of leading to the experimental conciliation of many paradoxes and putting an end to narrow-mindedness that provokes arguments about which is the "true" path. An additional result would be the spontaneous understanding of the essences of all religious traditions.

I have, up to now, developed my vision of what I call integral education, that is, an education of the body, emotions, mind and spirit, that is based on a balanced contemplation of its different aspects, and that can give the world beings capable of understanding this vision and serving it with generosity. What can we do in favor of such a noble initiative?

Of course, the decisive question is expanding and making this form of comprehension known. Greater progress in this comprehension on the part of everyone is susceptible to paving the way to later development, more creative than any produced to date in the area of private education, and that is something already.

The next step in making the dream reality resides, nevertheless, in educating educators.

Many educators have been doing this by themselves in a certain way. Guided by a hunger for personal growth and the love of their profession they find new experiences and information needed in different forms of self-directed continuous education. It is to be expected, however, that within a short period of time centers for formation of educators may have assimilated the holistic form of comprehension to which we have referred enough so that

when the educators leave the university they will have
developed, together with the maturity and depth necessary, the
perspective and the series of abilities that an integral education
requires.

After expansion and maturity of consciousness in the
population, and especially in professionals, will naturally
come the reform of the official educational system:  the
revolution of today is the "establishment" of tomorrow.
Social institutions possess their own characteristic inertia, and
growth takes place as a result of overcoming this inertia
through prospective vision: "the domesticating power of small
things" in the language of the *I-Ching*. The educational
establishment has been deservedly compared, because of its
inertia, to a white elephant, and the services that it offers are
obsolete and irrelevant to an absolutely unjustifiable point.
Indiscipline in schools, I'm sure, is in this sense a reactive
phenomenon, a type of strike against uselessness, an appeal
for an education that is relevant for our critical times and real
problems, an education that we can truly called wise and that
really helps us to be better.

I trust I have transmitted, in everything I've said, a
certain consciousness about the negativity and irrelevance of
our current educational system which is patriarchal and
archaic and anti-holistic with respect to the real human
situation today, and I hope to have made clear that this is a
topic that requires urgent attention.  Our education is absurd as
potentially "saving".  It is absurd to the point that many people
have talked about eliminating schools as we know them as the
most adequate solution (Ivan Illich considered dismantling
schools the fundamental step in the liberation process needed
from authoritarianism in general).  Many think that current
education, not only no longer performs the function it was
meant for, but by omission, has done damage.  On saying this,
I remember the image on a poster that showed a picture of a
group of very lively children next to another of a group of
people on a bus, with robotic faces and bored expressions.
The phrase below the pictures read, "What happened?"
Looking for an answer to this process of turning off, of the

dulling of human faculties, there is no doubt that the prize would have to go to an educational process like the one we have, so very opposite to the one we should be trying to achieve.

The global situation we are experiencing makes me think it is "urgent" and not only important to find a solution to this problem, since, in spite of the fact that the crisis we are going through is a consequence of the failure of our proposals in the area of human relations, we are totally ignoring learning in the transpersonal dimension in our educational environment.

After the expression "world problems," referring to the macro-problem that all problems that escape the capability of isolated specialists have been concentrated in, had circulated for many years, Alexander King, co-founder of the Club of Rome, established in his book *The First Global Revolution*, recently published, the new expression "resolutic" as a counterpart and, in his proposal of a complex way out of the situation, he emphasized the importance of education, along with technology. According to him, education should have the following objectives:

- Acquire knowledge
- Structure intelligence and develop critical faculties
- Develop self-knowledge and the consciousness of one's own talents and limitations
- Learn to overcome undesirable impulses and destructive behavior
- Permanently wake creative and imaginative faculties in the person
- Learn to play a responsible role in society
- Learn to communicate with others
- Help people to adapt to and prepare for change
- Allow each person the acquisition of a global concept of the world

• Form individuals that will be operative and capable of solving problems[4]

I personally celebrate and share King's declarations, but I feel that in his purely objective language, taken from the world of economy, politics and engineering, he has lost something substantially vital: I find the absence of words like "love" and "compassion" meaningful. They are words that our world, based on the development of the left hemisphere of the brain, considers implicitly forbidden, just like the characters of Aldous Huxley's *Brave New World* considered it bad taste to talk about the incubator.

I would like to make reference now to the fact that one of the reasons there has not been more advance up to now in formulating these additional objectives that education should pursue is the implicit conviction that trying to reach them will be excessively expensive. It seems natural to think that such a radical change in the objectives of education—not to mention the means involved in education—would require a corresponding change in the personnel in charge of reaching those goals.

But I believe the problem is not as unsolvable as it may appear. The definitive key, for example, would be a different pattern in the formation of educators who currently receive an excess of intellectual baggage and insufficient emotional and spiritual education. For example, in the area of psychology a lot is taught about behaviorism, but nothing that really helps to change people; in other words, they learn to change concrete behavior but not to change the way of life. Why? Because behaviorism is scientific and as such only occupies itself with what can be measured.

Once, one of the professors in medical school, Ignacio Matte-Blanco, Chilean psychoanalyst who immigrated to Italy years ago, told me that a friend of his had wanted to study medicine because he thought it was a vocation that treated the

---

[4]*The First Global Revolution* by Alexander King and Bertrand Schneider, Pantheon Books, 1991 (English language edition).

human being and that understood the human mind. With time, he realized how impossible creating an authentic science of the mind would be, and he dedicated his life to the study of the transmission of nervous impulses and the polarization of the neuronal axis membrane of the squid. I think that all of us have gone through that to some extent: since we are scientists we limit the field of our interests to what science includes and can measure, converting ourselves into prisoners of the patriarchal game, scientificism that is not, of course, the same as science but only a caricature of the scientific spirit.

The topic of economy can be looked at in this context, because I'm convinced that the needed change of direction in education is possible and easily within our reach, and that it would be far less expensive than what we would imagine. Just by having a sufficient level of consciousness, it would be a revolution as reachable as turning a switch on. Remember the analogy of the French Revolution, where a radical change in the orientation of education (from a humanistic approach to a scientific conception) was possible only because there was a strong government that was able to decide on the change. "Well," said the authorities, "let's bring scientists into the schools." People who understood science were those who worked in laboratories, like Lavoisier and his disciples. It was the era of the birth of science, and it brought to schools and to teaching people who had no pedagogical experience, but who had a lot to communicate.

I believe that now something similar needs to be done: give limited space to subjects that currently make up the programs (in reality the greater part of whatever we've learned we've learned outside of school), condense a large part of what is done today in schools and make room in schools for people that have been working on their own higher inner development, people involved in the growing experiential therapeutic and spiritual movement that is blossoming around us. This double angle of seeking (psychological and spiritual) is a response to the thirst for answers that has awakened in mankind when culture—our patriarchal culture is not only obsolete and in crisis, but agonizing—has no longer provided them. Nietzsche said a century ago that God was dead, but what he was referring to in reality was the image that mankind had formed of God in their minds: that image, so linked to the patriarchal mentality, has definitely died. For the spirit to be reborn, it is necessary to speak other languages, open up to the thirst and stop feeling separate from this concern that is so natural to mankind. And this is happening in our times. In a particularly genuine way, that search and that concern has characterized diverse groups and tendencies that are part of Humanistic Psychology, born in the USA as the "Human Potential Movement" in the 60's and developed later under the name of Transpersonal Psychology, that could well be considered an emerging new type of shamanism. It is a contagious process that overflows because of its own dynamism within the framework of academics, under its undeniable and vigorous ability to self-inseminate.

I think that within this general movement it would be good to recruit a sufficient number of psycho-spiritual educators, and educational institutions would do well in allowing them to participate in their work starting now, even if it were just experimentally and complementary. This would be a start, since the ideal and definitive change would require, as is logical, a new education for educators: life only begets life, and maturity only comes from people who have matured, especially when what is to be transmitted is an integral and strictly human formation.

What is being missed in schools that train educators today is a series of abilities and knowledge in the therapeutic and spiritual areas, when, in my opinion, it would be relatively inexpensive to include these teachings in the respective programs. I say this based on my own experience, since I have organized similar training programs, even though they have been directed toward therapists and not educators. I think that through intensive, brief programs that do not require excess time, it would be possible to offer effective help to educators that feel burned out, bored, incapable of truly relating to their students, unmotivated, and condemned to continue doing something they no longer believe in, not able to see a way out of the situation.

I have often had occasion to talk about this topic to chosen, specialized audiences, and I have always felt a resonance that makes me feel optimistic as to the spreading and propagation of the contents of the ideas set out. Among these opportunities, two have been especially significant.

One was held in the Second International Holistic Congress, in Belo Horizonte in 1991, where the audience unanimously passed a motion to recommend to the UNESCO to take into account the urgency of adding the emotional and spiritual factors to education.

The second was in the International Symposium on Mankind, celebrated in Toledo, Spain, also in 1991, during which I did a survey of the audience that attended my conference. Nearly half were educators and also on this occasion the answer was unanimous in support of my proposal in favor of a more holistic approach to education that would be nurtured by the contributions from the "Revolution of Consciousness" and the humanistic movement in general and that would favor the affective aspect and spiritual growth in students.

### 6.  A Curriculum for Self-knowledge, Interpersonal Re-education and Spiritual Cultivation

*"The question we must ask ourselves is "what?":    What subjects should we teach?    When the conversation becomes deeper, we start asking "how": What methods and techniques are needed for good teaching? Occasionally, we go even further and actually ask "why": What is the purpose and why do we teach? But we rarely ask "who": How can the quality of my being determine the way I relate to my students, my topic, my colleagues, my world?"*

G. Leonard, Op. cit.

It is customary for one to begin by saying one is very pleased to be with the people present, and in spite of the fact that I usually avoid conventional formulas, this occasion is so special for me that I cannot leave it out:  when I received Hugo Diamante's invitation by phone I told him that the topic of education motivates me, and now that I'm here I see that this is one of the liveliest congresses I've attended, both because of the declarations made and because of  the way these declarations are being received.  Also, I believe that at this age, I have something important to share with educators and I feel like someone who, without realizing it, has been working for many years on formulating something that suddenly seems to be a useful social invention in a way much different than I would have imagined.

Let me explain that better:  working on the formation of therapists I have perfected a very potent human development program that could well fill the gap that the formation of teachers so unfortunately suffers from in the area of self-knowledge, human relations and contemplative life.

I am going to follow the examples of some people who have spoken before me, like Dr. Janis Rozé and Fernando Flores, and in order to put the ideas I want to express into context, I will tell the story of the work I've been doing, which began as psychological and spiritual work with seekers and later became oriented toward the formation of therapists, and I suspect that it will reach its maximum utility as a complement to the current formation of teachers.

I can begin this story from the time when I traveled to California for the first time and went to the Esalen Institute. I was then a young psychiatrist who worked in a new department in the medical school of the University of Chile, the Center for Medical Anthropology Studies, which had the objective of mitigating the well-known process of dehumanization that traditional medical education produces in the students. But more so, I was what I have been for most of my life: a seeker.

Today the Esalen Institute is very well-known because of its notable history—intimately linked to that of Fritz Perls —and for its influence on a great number of therapeutic centers around the world. At its beginning during the 60's, the institute wished to implement an idea that Aldous Huxley described as teaching "non-verbal humanities." This required gathering diverse contributions to human development that at that time had come about independently, as did the diverse disciplines oriented toward body consciousness, group work oriented toward emotional consciousness, the application of art to self-knowledge, etc.

At Esalen I met people that became important in my life, like Perls and Simkin, Alan Watts and Joseph Campbell, but the stimulus that this novel center provided was also decisive in my conception of a school that, different from Esalen (a place where one went to participate in brief activities), would offer a true curriculum—a set of complementary disciplines that students could integrate into an original synthesis.

It began when I got back to Chile after being at Esalen, and even though the activity I developed did not make a name for itself locally, the catalog from Esalen made reference to it, using the expression Esalen-Chile and, upon my return later to the United States this work made up the germinal form of what I would do later there, as well as the life oriented basis for the book that I then wrote (*The Only Search*) about compared methodology and aspects underlying many spiritual and therapeutic paths.

Upon returning to the U.S.A., Esalen not only invited me as a Gestalt therapist, but also gave me the freedom to pursue my experimental initiative, and it was during this time that I most strongly felt that the influence received as a seeker and in professional life converged in my work. The combination of therapy and meditation took on special meaning—novel at that time; and particularly novel was that it was not only a simple juxtaposition between meditation and psychotherapy, but an effort to integrate them both: interpersonal exercises through which the meditative attitude could be transferred to situations involving verbal situations.

All this, however, was interrupted for more than a year by an experience that I can describe as the major pilgrimage of my life —when I left my home, my work and my plans for the future to join a spiritual teacher then unknown, in whom I recognized a link with the mysterious and remote spiritual tradition that had influenced me during my adolescence through Gurdjieff.

What began as a personal project was transformed into a new school—since when I asked Oscar Ichazo (the name of the teacher I am speaking of) if I could invite others (originally John Lilly, Ram Das, Stanley Keleman and John Bleibtreu) the project woke unsuspected interest in others and I ended up traveling to the oasis of Azapa (near Arica in the extreme northern part of Chile) with more than 40 others, many of them from Esalen.

To say that the experience for me had a profound spiritual impact is an understatement; it was in truth a birth to a level of consciousness previously unknown and the beginning of a path toward deep-seated transformation that had no going back. Naturally, this was reflected in my later work for which my entire life before now seemed to be only preparation.

For some years this work was concentrated on a group of some 60 people (in Berkeley) and took on the shape of continuous improvisation more than the implementation of a premeditated program. With time, however, a proper program was formed and for this I was lucky enough to have the collaboration of notable teachers like Rabbi Zalman Schachter, Dhiravamsa, the tantric master Harish Johari and Ch'u Fang Chu—disciple of the last Taoist patriarch, who came to California at that time from Taiwan.

So, a new school appeared again, and when it became necessary to give it a name (in order to establish a non-profit educational corporation) I called it SAT in triple reference to the Sanskrit words for Being and Truth, and the initials of Seekers After Truth and (using phonetic symbolism) a three-part vision of the mind and the things that transpire through the esoteric Christianity transmitted by Gurdjieff and Ichazo and that characterize my own understanding of psychic life.

In the same way that my work in Chile resulted in the base form of the work I would do later in the United States, my work on the SAT program in North America became the form of what, some 15 years later, I would use in Europe. It began with the invitation to preside over a summer course oriented toward "professional and personal orientation" for psychotherapists, and this was set up in a format of three sessions (one per year) that lasted one month each. Over time the format of the course has been reduced little by little and its current form has three modules of 10 days each.

The way in which a three-month program has become so much more compact, could never have been theoretically anticipated; only the evolution of a practice over time allows the expression of creativity in the course of an emerging process. So, over about 15 years and thanks to the evolution of these courses (more practical and experiential than theoretical) they seem to have taken on the form of something that I hope can serve to ferment transformation in the world of education, since it has helped a large number of therapists in diverse countries.

I wish to talk briefly now about the contents of the curriculum, predominantly experiential, that takes place with the help of valuable collaborators and has been refined progressively through the years, showing very satisfactory results.

The fundamental structure (that is the flag under which I have always worked) is the union of meditation and therapy, which is no longer as novel as it was when I introduced it in Esalen more than thirty years ago. In spite of the fact that many spiritual schools say that therapy is irrelevant, and that therapeutic schools consider spiritual issues an illusion or avoidance of reality ("the opiate of the masses"), I think that the interpersonal aspect of the mind and the transpersonal or spiritual aspect are no more than two aspects of the same phenomenon—and the cure found in emotional re-education (which is nothing more than the reestablishment of our loving capacity) is not separable from spiritual realization nor dispensable in the Great Journey of the soul.

The combination of meditation (the old contemplative path) and psychotherapy (the "interpersonal yoga" that makes up the main contribution from our culture to the path of self-realization) has a very particular strength. When I say meditation, I am not only referring to a large territory but a multifaceted reality, since meditation is the conjunction of many elements, some of which are more or less exalted in different cultures. My way of teaching meditation, as you will see, is integrative, although it does focus on the Buddhist contribution.

To talk about meditation in the larger meaning of the word practically coincides with talking about spirituality, since the technical differences in known forms of meditation make up the main spiritual exercises that humanity knows. When speaking of the spirit or of spirituality we sometimes only have a very vague or fragmented idea of what they are and a wider knowledge of meditation could be the best way of filling this lagoon in our education, since the spiritual dimension of life, like meditation, is multifaceted and each of the aspects makes up an access route to that depth of the mind that is sometimes simply referred to as "higher consciousness."

When the western world says that spiritual consciousness is important, what we are basically saying is that the sense of the divine or orientation toward the divine is important. As a result of the confusion between the experience of the divine and ideology or simple belief, however, just as of the growing secularization of beliefs, we could say that the spiritual ideal once conceived has lost validity, and that the traditional forms of prayer are considered by many to be a residual of past superstitions. That is why it seems important to me to rescue the experiential aspect of the divine that does not depend on any ideology or on a theistic vision of the world; its essence is the basis of what is sacred, and it is cultivated through a type of meditation that directs the attention toward symbolic contents that have the purpose of evoking a supreme value. (Although that supreme value is not found necessarily in the objects or qualities, we could say that it could be projected on images, sounds, colors and even concepts—such as the "I." nothingness, supreme consciousness or the divine.)

But, as intrinsic as the sacralizing capacity of spiritual maturity can be and as desirable as "re-enchantment with the world" through cultivating this maturity can be, we must not confuse the sense of that sacred and even less the intuition of a transcendent divinity with the spiritual, since these are facets or manifestations of the Spirit. The learning implied in a form of meditation in which a person, apparently, does the opposite of evoking sacredness is equally relevant to higher consciousness, since it does not attend to symbolic contents but to the sensorial and, instead of generating an experience of the mysterious supreme value that envelops the world of things without belonging to it, directs the intent on simple or pure perception of the "here and now", as is typical of Theravada Buddhism.

In both cases, meditation is related to orientation of attention. It can lead to the "immediate consciousness information" that Bergson spoke of (what I can touch, what I can see, what I can hear, emotions, here and now body sensations) which we can consider the surface of consciousness (and it is very important that we recover the ability to contact with the immediate, that we once had as children and perhaps have lost since we are too immerse in our symbolic world), or toward the depth of the mind that is the seat of the experience of the self, of the "I" and of the divine. And this depth of the mind is not available through ordinary consciousness; however, it can be evoked or invoked, by times, through the type of meditation we have referred to, in which we concentrate on symbolic material that works toward the development of creative imagination and the evoking of meaning—with the characteristic result being the experience of the sacred.

These two aspects of meditation are aspects that are complementary to life in general and it is convenient to observe how they become particularly present in psychotherapy, without this meaning that they are more relevant in the therapeutic area than in education. We know all too well how an important aspect of therapy is precisely recovering the capacity to be "present" or to be in the "here and now" as so frequently has been stated since the times of Fritz Perls.

Today Perls is remembered as the creator of a therapeutic system but we don't know to what degree he can be seen as a prophetic figure due to the impact that he had on society in his days; we could say that he was the prophet of the here and now and that through his personal impact he made those who knew him feel that he represented a path to presence, a path to personal development that held the capacity to have an attitude that the past no longer exists and the future is still not here (at this moment we won't delve so deeply as to begin to doubt the future as well). If we adopt the attitude of taking the present as the only thing that exists, that will take us to a deeper experience of the moment, more remote and at the same time richer than we are accustomed to believe. It then will seem as if we have lost the capacity to make contact with the experience of the moment, and admit it and confess it. How many times, in the course of a conversation have we felt bored, upset, or unhappy with what is happening without knowing how to get out of the situation, when the way to get out is in being able to simply say: "At this moment I don't like what is happening"; or "I don't know what is happening, but there is something I don't like." This freedom in itself to talk about the experience of the moment, no matter how vaguely, will change the course of the conversation. But we don't think that the rules of society allow speaking about what is happening at the moment; or, if we explore the issue, we find difficulties.

It is precisely this contact with the present, together with the communication of the present experience that changed the spirit of contemporary therapies when it permeated them. Before that, psychoanalysis had invited us to reflect on the past, on what happened in childhood as the origin of psychological problems. Reich began to observe more what was happening in the present and Perls was the person who paid even more attention to it, even proposing that it would be enough to work with the present, recovering the capacity and the right to feel what one feels, to know what one feels, to know what one thinks, to know what one is doing, to be able to realize the obvious. But just as the recovery of the quality of the experience is important, we could say that pathology has its roots in this loss of capacity to know what we feel and that what we call unconscious resides in not having the right to realize what is happening to us which goes hand in hand with being accomplices in a social lie.

But just as the person who meditates does not always focus his attention on the experience of the moment, in the therapeutic world, where language is used as a tool, not only is it important to recover the simple present. It is also important to recover the magic dimension of life, and when we talk about the transpersonal aspect in psychotherapy it has a lot to do with the recovery of the things that are found in the religious conceptions of the world, disdained by the scientific attitude of newly born psychology: spiritual teachings, myths, and fairy tales that, like fingers that point toward the moon, should not be confused with the moon itself. In them there is a recurrence of symbolic language in order to go beyond the symbolic—to the center of the mind itself—to evoke something that transcends specific contents of the mind and that we can conceive as consciousness itself, the divine essence of the mind and the source of sacredness.

I have stated that spiritual development is multifaceted and that relevant to it is the cultivation of religious sentiment, like the cultivation of the attention to immediate reality that doesn't seem so spiritual from a traditional Christian perspective. Another path to access spiritual maturity (that we introduce in the second module of the program, after beginning with Vipassana) is represented by forms of meditation that work on stopping the mind in order to transcend it. This is done, in turn, through concentration.

Traditional teachings from different cultures tell us that only when the mind is still can it reflect something that is beyond it. We need to inhibit our passional mind and the inner voices that come from the ego, inhibit our neurotic needs and learn in that way to hold our thoughts in pacific silence.

But if meditation is to know how to be still, it is also true that it is the opposite; or better said, complementary: to allow the mind to flow.

There are various complementarities in the mind, and meditation can only be explained paradoxically. It is like having one foot in each aspect of the paradox in order to peek into another dimension, just as practices in which attention is directed to the surface of the mind or, alternatively, to its mysterious depths (through symbolic representations), as occurs in cultivating stillness and that aspect of meditation that consists in educating inner spontaneity: allowing the mind to go where it will, loosening limiting voluntary control. Of course the paradox is such that when one loosens control on one's own mental processes, it is probable that they will be still, and the opposite also happens; if one truly knows how to be still, something analogous to what happens when a person is on a rowboat and stops rowing happens; the water carries the boat and its passenger. And if we allow ourselves to be carried, currents of one's being that are ever more subtle and deep will be felt. And just as when students in a classroom stop talking and can listen to the teacher, inside ourselves, if the small voices are quiet, a voice from a different level can be heard. And vice versa: when our deeper mind is made manifest it is easier to be still. This can be taken even to a solemn moment in our development: when a new level of life begins to express itself in us and what we then realize is banal and trivial begins to die in us.

These two aspects of meditation—stillness and spontaneity—have to do with action, and the respective instructions can be compared to the red and green traffic lights, with their stop and go meanings. Of course, both stillness and spontaneity are aspects of life that deserve to be appreciated and cultivated and are, as well, components of psychotherapy.

It can be said that many psychotherapeutic theories formulated by the founders of traditional schools, are formulated around certain ideas that are more or less true but that do not provide a universal explanation. If we look for an all-encompassing trans-systemic theory of psychotherapy, certainly one of the general principles that we can find is precisely the cultivation of deep spontaneity, allowing one to flow. Whether it is Moreno's psychodrama, which worked explicitly on cultivating spontaneity, or free association in psychoanalysis or encounter groups, it is obviously this that is in play: deconstructing so that when superficial thought and communication patterns are broken down, deeper structures are allowed to surface and less obvious truths can blossom.

This is especially apparent in Gestalt which is an important manifestation of the Dionysian spirit in the contemporary world—of the spirit that implies faith in the spontaneous and natural, and that Nietzsche proclaimed as the only salvation possible for our western culture (so devitalized and dehumanized by the effects of millenniums of religious authoritarianism and its "enslaving" morals). Besides having an important Gestalt component, the SAT program includes two elements that are especially useful for education of spontaneity: a combination of psychological exercises based on free association of ideas (that I have described in my book *In Meditation as in Psychotherapy*), and a new discipline that has come from the area of dance: "Authentic Movement" that was originally designed by Mary Whitehouse.

Just as I have countered the "stop" and "go" of meditation and described a polarity between the inner gestures of paying attention to the sacred depths of the mind or to the concrete contents of the same, we can also understand the affective dimension of the mind (not any less relevant to meditation) in terms of complementariness. Many forms of meditation are based on detachment: stepping back, unidentifying with what is happening, with what one is feeling or desiring. We take ourselves too seriously, we could say we are too immersed in our pain or in our preferences, in our opinions and especially in our scars—in other words in the aftertaste of what happened to us at some point in time and that is still affecting us like a shadow or ghost, separating us from the present. What the Orientals call karma is nothing more than the weight of the past on the present (that does not necessarily come from other lives). In view of the attachment that characterizes our habitual state (and more so our emotional perturbations) we need to take a step back, sometimes using humor, and sometimes simply in a serene way. Naturally, such a "philosophical attitude," characteristic of wisdom, can be reached over time through life experience, but it is an intrinsic part of certain practices of meditation whose fruit is what I have called "cosmic indifference."

Even though one ideal of life is to reach a loving attitude, love and detachment are not incompatible; not only are they not opposites, but they also make up a mysterious complementary combination: it is easier to become loving if we are capable of detachment, since one cannot give of oneself if one is too attached to what one is or has. And it is also difficult to reach detachment without a generous attitude, without enthusiasm, love of life, love of others, or love of something. This complementary attitude is similar to that of life and death, which are so intertwined in certain literary works.

If therapy has more to do with love, meditation points more toward detachment, but it is also true that in therapeutic theory as in meditational theory we need to take into account both issues and understand their complementarity.

The idea that mental silence or unidentification with passions (detachment) can be fundamental capacities of mankind and an important path toward spiritual consciousness is far from our educational practices. And how much farther yet we are from taking the capacity to surrender ourselves to the solicitations or subtle voices of our inner world seriously — our capacity for surrender, for tuning into the depth of life, in agreement with its totality! Today we have barely proposed combining instruction with "education in values" but in practice it has only meant, in the best of cases, an evaluation of values. The capacities that I propose as essential facets of spiritual life require, on the contrary, much more enthusiasm and rhetoric: cultivated through a transforming process that requires the presence of guides who, through the corresponding discipline, have achieved them in themselves.

More can be said of the aspect of meditation that is geared toward developing the capacity to sacralize, that seems to have become irrelevant in our disenchanted postmodern world. Were the religious geniuses of humanity simply dreaming when they recommended the love of God as the most important of precepts? I suspect, instead, that the collective deterioration of consciousness is a result of our excessively mercantile spirit, which does not like to hear about values that can compete with earnings.

And I'll leave the topic of meditation here and go on to consider the therapeutic element that forms part of this human development curriculum that I am proposing as a complement to the current formation of educators. When I announce the program as a curriculum (supplementary) of "self-knowledge, interpersonal re-education and spiritual cultivation" I have implicitly referred to the therapeutic area through two intimately connected enterprises: self-knowledge or insight, and promoting a voluntary change in human relations. And in that way, even though I've said that the SAT program combines meditation and psychotherapy, it is more exact to say that it combines meditation, self-knowledge and interpersonal repairing.

I'll begin by explaining what I mean by self-knowledge as the objective of the so-called insight psychotherapies or "deep therapy."

Self-knowledge has always been recognized as a path to transformation. We profess a certain collective veneration of the "know thyself" that we associate with the figure and mission of Socrates and the oracle of Delphos; but in this we are collective hypocrites. If we were not, self-knowledge would have a fundamental place in our educational practice.

People who suffer psychologically, in other words, those who cannot cease their emotional problems, have discovered that they need self-knowledge to correct their dysfunctional state, and the need for a collective cure has fueled the development of the new path of transformation that is modern psychology.

While traditional spiritual schools have taken on the work of overcoming the ego through the practice of virtuous conduct and spiritual contemplation, psychotherapy expects that in the first place the transcendence of childhood conditioning will come through the understanding of oneself. And although it could be argued that psychotherapy has shed much less light on the world than the great religions with their saints and prophets have, its contribution cannot be denied as it has been formidable and indispensable in our times.

The enterprise that is geared toward self-understanding holds diverse facets:

1. Contacting one's own experience in the here and now, which implies not only the capacity for accepting and recognizing one's own experience and cultivating the practice of meditation (specifically the techniques of Vipassana), but an education in the capacity to be a witness to one's self, in other words, to live with the

most consciousness possible instead of living life on "automatic pilot".

2. Retrospection, which means contacting past experience through memory. This retrospective clarification is stimulated and facilitated, in turn, by expression, whether it be through writing or oral communication. In our program writing is at the service of the comprehension of life, on one hand, and on the other, there is systematic oral communication through free association in a meditative context that serves to clarify and analyze daily experience.

3. Another facet of self-knowledge is the comprehension of the moment in the context of the total experience. Self-comprehension goes further than knowing what is felt and thought in a determined moment: what in psychology is called insight implies the organization of our self-observations into a coherent configuration, which implies understanding, for example, the repetitive patterns in our relationships as well as how our present experiences are related to past ones. It implies, also, understanding our personality and how it influences our lives. The greatest stimulus for self-comprehension is found in a dialog with those, who in virtue of their own self-knowledge are capable of understanding what is going on inside us. In the SAT program, this dialog is held within the context of diverse interpersonal psychological exercises and in therapeutic workshops with Gestalt therapists and other professionals.

4. To all that has been said we must add an additional component in the process of self-knowledge that is the clarification of understanding through theoretical formulations or maps of reference. Each psychological school interprets individual experiences based on a different theory and the one we use for support is none of the ones known in the academic world, but a vision of the psyche developed based on an esoteric inspiration from central Asia.

The psychological map that is the most satisfactory and clarifying that I have seen up to now is not any of the proposals from academic psychology, but one that has come to us from an Asian esoteric tradition that I have developed into what I call "the Psychology of the Enneatypes." I am referring to the application of the Enneagram to the study of the personality—something that has, up to now, seen little resonance in the professional world, perhaps because the abundant literature produced by those who wish to make it known has left so much to be desired that popular enthusiasm for the topic has been interpreted by academics as a sign of mediocrity.

It was Gurdjieff who introduced the Enneagram in the West, and whoever wishes to know more about his thoughts on it can find information in a very interesting book by a Russian newspaperman of his time—Ouspensky—*In Search of the Miraculous.*

Although Gurdjieff was one of the main influences in my life, the psychological aspects of the Enneagram were something I learned from a Bolivian who I have mentioned in reference to my year-long pilgrimage in Arica: Oscar Ichazo, who, using the name protoanalysis, presented to the college of psychologists in Chile in 1969 a set of notions in which could be heard an echo of a continuation of the very old Christian tradition of capital sins; even though it was many centuries ago that what was practical psychology in the times of the Fathers of the Desert and today survives as dogma in the church was lost as living knowledge in the West.

In our times we can reformulate the doctrine of capital sins by saying that, although we have all suffered a lack of love in childhood in a greater or lesser fashion, we have developed in a specific way to try to get what we were lacking; and so, for example, we have developed a passion for applause, for recognition, for intensity, to be loved, and so on. Definitively: we have learned maneuvers designed to get love and I have never seen a better map for understanding the variety of these maneuvers than the map of the Enneagram, coherent with the one Dante followed when classifying sinners in hell or in purgatory. For some, the fundamental dynamic is pride, for others envy, etc., and there are psychologists who have shown interest mainly in one or another of the basic emotions (such as the interest Melanie Klein showed in envy, the interest of Karen Horney in pride as the center of understanding of everything psychic; or Freud who centered on anxiety and fear). But the Enneagram allows us to have a global vision of all of the human types and we can begin to see that there is not one psychology, but nine: each one with its implicit insanity, its dysfunctional ideas and its own exaggerated needs.

Going on to talk about interpersonal education that, more than any other aspect of education, necessarily implies relearning, repairing relationships, and work aimed at changing conducts, we can say that, as in the case of self-understanding, this re-education goes further than formulas or techniques in presenting potential at each moment of our lives.

In the curriculum of the SAT program, an especially important component in this purpose of repair is the work destined to the recovery of the original loving bond with parents. I developed this work many years ago, inspired by the work that was being done individually by an American clairvoyant, Robert Hoffman, who then refined the group process that I proposed, giving birth to the "Hoffman Process of the Quadrinity."

I have included in this book a chapter written years ago about Hoffman and his therapeutic process in *The Agony of the Patriarchy* bringing attention to the potential that this notable contribution has in the re-education of our capacity to love for future education, so I'll only say here that although the process we use in the SAT program is not identical to the one offered by the Hoffman International Institute, the basic ideas are the same. Since the loving bond with mother and father are affected in most individuals because of interference by resentment, whether conscious or unconscious, it requires healing, and this in turn requires consciously feeling the pain and the catharsis of repressed anger. Only in this way can we reach, through comprehension and compassion, forgiveness and spontaneous benevolence.

Of all the rest of our relationships none is often more important than our couple's relationship, and these loving relationships also receive special attention in the SAT program through a course dedicated to taking advantage of difficulties in couples' relationships for personal evolution. And to complement the work mentioned there are others that attend to the elaboration of pending interpersonal situations—through Gestalt and integrative psychotherapy workshops.

The program offers ample opportunity to experiment with Gestalt therapy and learn it, so much so that that it has provoked interest as a course for perfecting the abilities of many already formed Gestalt therapists. This emphasis on a determined psychotherapeutic school could well be attributed to an era in which psychotherapeutic schools have multiplied and Gestalt has lost the prominence it had three decades ago, but even though Gestalt is one of my specialties, I believe that the election of this type of therapy (over NLP or TA, for example) is completely justified because of its universality, it usefulness for eclectic therapists and, particularly, because of its relevance in education.

Precisely because Gestalt is a very plastic tool that is at the same time a very creative way to work with the emotional aspects of life, it has been chosen as the therapeutic complement most relevant for instruction by George Brown, who decades ago was dean of the School of Education for the University of California at Santa Barbara. Brown was the founder, many years ago (with the support of the Ford Foundation), of a project called Confluent Education, in which Gestalt was adopted for teacher preparation so that they would have, together with the capacity to teach, the ability to deal with what happens humanly in the here and now, in themselves and in their students. In order to, for example, ask someone who has a disgusted look on his face what is wrong without being afraid of not knowing what to do with the reality of the experience. This implies a formation (characteristically set off by Gestalt) that allows the educator to enter into a true encounter; to be able to make a parenthesis in the process of instruction when it is needed in order to attend to the affective, interpersonal reality of the moment.

I want to underline the relevance of Gestalt therapy in education by pointing out that when Perls taught in the USA through Esalen Institute, many times he didn't announce his workshops as psychotherapy, but as "education in expressivity," "education of attention," "education of presence," etc., etc. The capacity that Gestalt wishes to educate is so universal that we don't even appreciate it really: knowing what is happening and being able to "be here." Nevertheless, it is so difficult that only experienced seekers, people who have a certain path traveled, duly appreciate and completely comprehend what it means to cultivate presence. Many times I ask people in groups that I work with, "What are you looking for?", "What have you achieved?", "Where are you?" And I find that only the most mature individuals answer that their efforts are to be more present.

The integrative psychotherapy laboratory that I have mentioned is one of the most significant and original aspects of the SAT program. In it the participants quickly acquire a capacity for helping that is not supported by theoretical knowledge, but by experience, by the comprehension that results in human capabilities such as listening, understanding what is said and desiring good for the other person. Besides the benefits that this can bring to others, the therapeutic exercises of the apprentices during the entire series that make up this practical program have resulted in noticeable benefits within the group itself, structured in such a way that each person gives and receives therapy from another person in the group in a supervised context. Beyond the therapeutic benefit that each member of the group reports from this situation, the experience of this laboratory—with its group sessions for comments that promote a generalized climate of transparency —contributes significantly to the formation of a true community. And in this way, frequently, at the end of the program, people who share their retrospective impressions say that their lives will never be the same after being so accepted, taken in, understood and loved by the group.

This aspect of the program seems to me to be one of my most novel and surprising contributions because of its effectiveness, in spite of the fact that during the steps in its formulation, far from feeling original, I was barely trying to establish exercises inspired by the most universal aspects of psychotherapy. Only having realized that there is no other program (that I know of) that is so brief and effective, has it seemed to me to be original, and it is clear that the center of this originality is found in the fact that psychotherapy can be learned with nothing more than brief theoretical or technical formulations—by following Rogers's proposal that says that the determining aspects in therapeutic activity are empathy, benevolence and authenticity.

It seems to me that psychotherapy has become very complicated; it has been mystified by bringing to the forefront things that are not fundamental. And I think that the fundamental factors of good psychotherapy are mainly personal, and not technical or theoretical. Perhaps the most important is that the therapist understands what is happening to the other person; if the therapist understands what is happening to the other, it is not necessary for the person to even say it, because of the almost magical effect that this has: the other intuitively knows that the therapist knows and he feels understood.

It is also important that the therapist is interested in the good of the other person, that the therapist is benevolent. And that will also be felt, independently of being expressed with words like, "Yes, I'm with you, I'm listening," or of not being expressed; perhaps it is even in better taste not to express something that is already understood. Authenticity is equally as important; therapy is done for truth, and through the calling out of the other person's truth.

But these three things—the capacity of the therapist to be authentic in order to induce authenticity in the other person; the capacity of the therapist to be interested in the other person; and the capacity of the therapist to understand the other person—are all things that are not cultivated in universities. They are not cultivated by reading books or in technical laboratories: they are cultivated through personal process, and I think it is time to change direction.

I have listed some of the influences that are strongly felt in the SAT program—like Gurdjieff, Ichazo, Perls, Hoffman and Rogers—but I haven't mentioned that a large part of the meditation teaching in the successive modules of the program follow the three fundamental traditions of Buddhism: the ancient Theravada tradition (represented mainly by Vipassana), Mahayana (represented by Zen Buddhism) and Vajrayana or Tibetan Buddhism. It is precisely the pedagogical conception of the Nyingmapa School of Tibetan Buddhism that is the inspiration for the meditation program as a whole—from beginning with Vipassana, continuing on with Shamata or the pacification of the mind as a basis for experiential exploration into the essence of consciousness, and having been a disciple of a highly creative teacher—Tarthang Tulku Rinpoche—I have also allowed myself a certain creativity in areas related to other aspects of meditation (like visualization, devotion, and the development of compassion) by replacing the traditional forms with novel applications using music, as could be expected of the applications of meditation and psychotherapy by someone who was a musician before he was a doctor—which explains why another component felt throughout the SAT program is music.

It would be too long to explain each of the elements that make up the SAT program here. Some of the ones I've mentioned are original and would be topics for books of their own—for example the psychotherapeutic laboratory that I've designed not only for training purposes, but as a way to set up a self-repairing group system. Another discipline that has come up in the development of our courses—as an encounter between my initiative and the ability of some collaborating disciples—has been a form of therapeutic drama that integrates the element of Gestalt and the psychology of the Enneatypes.

An additional component has been body-working psychotherapy, with its essence in body consciousness that results in correction of posture and improved fluidity in movement, with abundant psychological and spiritual implications. Throughout many years of experimenting, I have used a great variety of elements that go from yoga and tai-chi to Eutony, favoring, in more recent years, the Rio Abierto Method and Authentic Movement. Also part of the area of body-working psychology is an element developed by Mexican disciples (Chalakani and Kretzschmar) that combines "rebirthing" with regression to states that Grof called "perinatal wombs."

I'll close my comments on the main components of the SAT program here—comments that, naturally, are not sufficient to really provide an idea of how they work together to generate, when set into movement, a process of fertile interactions, and a resulting system that is alive and goes much further than its parts. From a different point of view, I could have talked about this process in terms of "an ego crushing machine", an initiation on the path to spontaneous development that is part of what we are beyond all ideology, or a living school whose essence is found more in the people who teach than in the explicit curriculum.

There are those who have referred to the SAT school as a school of love, as a place where one learns to be more human and more real. For many, it has been a discovery of the spiritual dimension of life. A large number of participants leave behind old ways of feeling and seeing things and feel that their lives take on a new course—or a change of course. It is, for most people, a gateway to the path of transformation and for those who are most committed it flows into a considerable distance on that same path.

An important aspect of the SAT program is the psychosocial nature: the group of participants becomes a true group where each one shows himself, explores alternative conducts and discovers that he is accepted and loved beyond his habitual roles. But the SAT process is not only a process in which people feel validated and accepted, there is also a strong element of confrontation, and I would say a good balance of nutrition and the proposed "holy war against the ego."

On occasions I have invited a group of colleagues to share what the SAT experience has meant to them and I have noticed the emphasis that they put on how it has been a gift for the participants to have as examples teachers who are "working on themselves" instead of hiding behind a professional role.

Today we amply recognize that psychotherapy depends more on the relationship than on the technique or even insight, that what it is about in the end is the benevolence of the therapist that allows him to "contain" his patients in a way the patient's parents were not able to. There is, however, a secondary recognition of the therapeutic value of authenticity that seems to me to be a fundamental ingredient in this living school.

It has been repeatedly observed that the therapeutic process offered in the SAT program is interesting and useful for high-level and beginning therapists, and that each of the courses is "almost a miracle" because of all the things that happen and all the things that people learn. I believe that it truly is and I consider this success an experimental confirmation of my inspirational conviction: that in order to help others we don't need extensive studies. We need our own experience of our own inner journey through self-knowledge and the efforts made: a relevant practical-experiential training, a clear vision of certain fundamental things and the capacity to be with a patient. Because of the prominence of this in the educational practice that I've designed we often talk about learning thanks to "healing through truth".

I'd like to close with the consideration of how our sick world in crisis needs the support of individual transformation: a healthy society is made up of healthy individuals and we cannot expect that the need for self-realization will be satisfied more than partially by traditional methods. It would be desirable to democratize psychotherapy or, more amply, an education in how to do spiritual and psychological work on oneself and how to help each other to do this.

It would be difficult to expect the world to improve without changing our education, making it relevant for psycho-spiritual development. And to change education we have to inject something new into the forming of educators.

I have explained how the SAT Institute came about in answer to the interest of a group of seekers in California in the 70's, and how it was reborn years later in Europe, in answer to the interest of therapists. Many educators have attended the courses, but only lately have institutions become interested, which fills me with joy because it seems to me that I have developed something that, through use by educators, holds great promise for the public; and I dream of the day my "invention" can contribute to a more favorable world for those who come after us.

I imagine that most people would agree that, if we want a different world, we won't get it just through politics, or merely through isolated individual spiritual or therapeutic progress. Not even through independent psycho-spiritual formation of teachers: it will be necessary to have the commitment of universities and financing for programs geared to teams of teachers from specific schools, so that by forming true groups they build a favorable atmosphere for the exercising of capacities currently not taken advantage of by teachers, as well as of free expression and development of students.

I know from many teachers that have gone through our program that this isn't happening now. They say that in spite of the great personal benefit that the program held for them and the new capacities they have developed for assisting others, what they've learned and experienced is of little use when they get back to their classrooms. And I don't doubt that many have shown in the course of group work great therapeutic capacity, having developed—through formation or because of innate talent—a notable ability to help in the development of others; but they feel that the environment of schools is not compatible with the complete expression of humanity and that it is not convenient to show their abilities, as if the system were at war with consciousness.

I suspect that, in spite of being an aberration that is barely visible to public consciousness, the failure of education is the greatest tragedy of our time. We criticize capitalism and the industrial military complex, and this is all well and good, but we would have to also blame the invisible partner of the military and industrial complex, the institutional inertia of the educational system.

This is tragic, because education, of all human institutions, must be responsible for caring for human development. And not only are we going through a historical moment in which our psycho-spiritual paralysis has become critical, but that above and beyond this, we are in the world to blossom and give fruit; in other words to develop our consciousness.

Should we be surprised then that our under-development in the subject of our humanity is expressed in a never ending list of disturbances and symptoms?

Those who have read my book *The Agony of the Patriarchy* are acquainted with my opinion that the universal crisis that characterizes our times, affecting from finances to ecology and the quality of life, is in essence a crisis caused by scarcity of love and wisdom—which is equivalent to saying a lack of attention to our development. Educators seem to have good intentions, but their efforts hide the institutional resistance to radical change. In Chile I was the private secretary to the minister of health at the beginning of my career, and I realize how easy it is to get lost in politics even when you have the best of intentions. It is convenient to remember that, just as individual pathology exists, there is also pathology in systems; a kind of spirit of the system, or malign social ego. And as in the case of the individual ego, its destructiveness lies in its lack of consciousness. As Cicero observed (although I don't remember his exact words): Each senator is a great man, but the senate as a group is a collective idiot. So, and in spite of the many politicians who have the best of intentions, politics is an infernal machine and even the best intentions are insufficient to move mountains.

Perhaps it is the same with education, I don't know. But the institutional inertia that makes education an enormous "white elephant" is larger and above all much more frightening than we imagine, and the fact that this "bureaucratic inertia" seems not to exist makes it even more powerful

I think that the general public and students especially should adopt a revolutionary attitude, since there is no other choice. I hope that all of us together can exert influence so that authorities embark on another path. Education is meant for human development, even though it has been used for other things as well, and even when our pseudo-democratic plutocracy demands education for automatic docility and production, I believe that an education for free realization of our evolutionary and creative potential can be critical for our collective survival.

## Publisher Contact Information

The publishers of this book invite you to contact the author via Gateways Books or (in Europe) via the Claudio Naranjo Institute:

Fundación Claudio Naranjo
calle Zamora 46-48, 6° 3ª
08005 Barcelona
Phone: +34 932097938
Email: info@fundacionclaudionaranjo.com

If you are interested in further reading along these lines, you may contact the publisher (contact information follows) or check the website for current books in the Consciousness Classics series:
Gateways Books and Tapes
PO Box 370-CE
Nevada City, CA 95959
(USA)
Email: info@gatewaysbooksandtapes.com
Phone: (530) 271-2239 or (800) 869-0658 (in the U.S.A.)
Website: www.gatewaysbooksandtapes.com

## Gateways Books by Claudio Naranjo:

*Character & Neurosis: An Integrative View*
*Catalyst of Miracles: The Unknown Claudio Naranjo*
    (festschrift)
*The Divine Child and the Hero: Inner Meaning in Children's*
    *Literature*
*The Enneagram of Society: Healing the Soul to Heal the*
    *World*
*Ennea-type Structures: Self-Analysis for the Seeker*
*Healing Civilization* (with Rose Press)
*The One Quest: A Map of the Ways of Transformation*

## Gateways Consciousness Classics - A Partial List of Titles You Can Order

by Salvatore Brizzi
*Draco Daatson's Book: The Never-Asleep Society Revealed*
  (translated from the Italian)

by Robert S. de Ropp
*The Master Game: Pathways to Higher Consciousness*
*Self-Completion: Keys to a Meaningful Life*
*Warrior's Way: A Twentieth Century Odyssey*

by Kyle Fite
*Orbit: An Introduction to the Principles and Practices of*
        *Bardo-Gaming on the Prosperity Path*

by E.J. Gold
*Alchemical Sex*
*American Book of the Dead*
*The Great Adventure: Talks on Death, Dying and the Bardos*
*The Human Biological Machine as a Transformational*
        *Apparatus*
*Parallel Worlds Explored*
*Practical Work on Self*
*The Hidden Work*
*Spiritual Gaming*
*Tarot Decoded*
*The Seven Bodies of Man*
*Visions in the Stone: Journey to the Source of Hidden*
        *Knowledge* (Intro. by Robert Anton Wilson)

By Barbara Haynes
*Every Day a Holy Day: Exercises, Experiments and Practices*
        *for Mindful Living*

by Michael Hutchison
*The Book of Floating: Exploring the Private Sea*

by Ka-Tzetnik 135633
*Shivitti: A Vision*

by Dr. John C. Lilly
*The Deep Self: Consciousness Exploration in the Isolation Tank*
*The Mind of the Dolphin: A Nonhuman Intelligence*
*Tanks for the Memories: Floatation Tank Talks* (with E.J. Gold)

by Dr. Claude Needham, Ph.D.
*The Original Handbook for the Recently Deceased*
*Just Because Club: Your Metaphysical Fitness Trainer*
*The Any Game Cookbook: Recipes for Spiritual Gaming*

by Mark Olsen
*The Golden Buddha Changing Masks: An Opening to Transformative Theatre*

By OM C. Parkin
*The Birth of the Lion: Non-Duality as a Way of Life*

by Kelly Rivera
*Journey to the Heart of the Maker*